The
Kensington Runestone

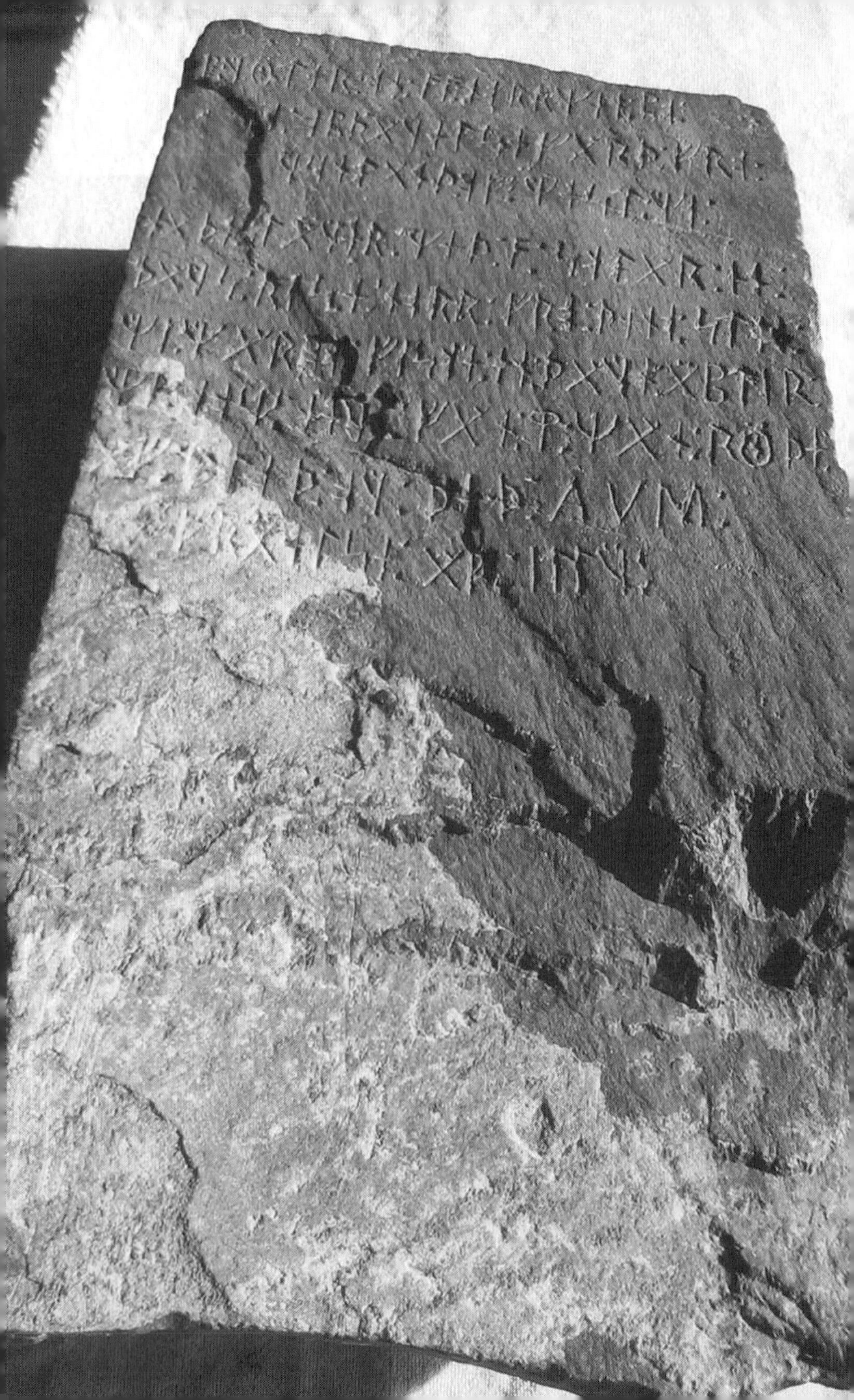

The Kensington Runestone

Approaching a Research Question Holistically

Alice Beck Kehoe

University of Wisconsin—Milwaukee

WAVELAND

PRESS, INC.

Long Grove, Illinois

For information about this book, contact:
Waveland Press, Inc.
4180 IL Route 83, Suite 101
Long Grove, Illinois 60047-9580
(847) 634-0081
info@waveland.com
www.waveland.com

Photos on cover, frontispiece, and page x by Scott Wolter.

Contents

Acknowledgements   v

Introduction   1

1   Farmer Ohman's Find   **3**

2   The Controversy   **11**

3   What Can Archaeology Show?   **21**

L'Anse aux Meadows   23

Archaeological Evidence for
   Norse and English in Arctic Canada   27

4   The Hard Data: Geology   **31**

5   Linguistics: Recognizing   **39**
   Medieval Dialect Variation

6   Biology: Tuberculosis?   **51**
   Blond Mandans? Red-haired Giants?

Tuberculosis in the American
   Midwest around A.D. 1000   52

"Blond Mandan"   55

Red Horn and Red-Haired Giants   58

Conclusion   60

7   The Norse   **63**
The Fur Trade   65

8   On the American Side   **71**
Was There a Fur Trade
in the Fourteenth Century?   73

Does the Kensington Runestone
Rewrite American History?   77

9   The Significance of the   **79**
Kensington Runestone

Sources   89
Bibliography   91
Index   101

Acknowledgments

I am grateful to Dick Nielsen, Barry Hanson, and Scott Wolter for including me in the teamwork that has made the Kensington Runestone question so intriguing. It has been a true pleasure to associate with such straightforward scientists. They generously sent me publications and papers without which this book could not have been written, and amplified these with many telephone conversations. Thanks, guys!

Right behind Dick, Barry, and Scott come my comrades in archaeology and ethnohistory, Helen Hornbeck Tanner, Guy Gibbon, and Dale Henning. That these scholars see the data as I do has been substantially encouraging. Larry Zimmerman for once didn't see eye to eye with me, but we had good discussions; maybe seeing the argument laid out here will satisfy him. Mike Michlovic has been stubborn but willing to talk it out. Birgitta Wallace extended the hand of friendship, and we hope will see how her researches in Newfoundland—the butternut she recognized at L'Anse aux Meadows—indirectly support the Kensington case. Robert Johnson and Tom Reiersgord have been actively interested Minnesotans, and my friends in NEARA, particularly Roz Strong, Sue Carlson, and Don Gilmore, keep issues alive in the Northeast. Jim Guthrie is another scientist whose collegial contributions I greatly appreciate.

Chapters have been read in draft by Wendy Leeds-Hurvitz and Bruno Giletti, giving me helpful comments. I've presented papers on the Runestone at American Society for Ethnohistory, Central States Anthropological Society, Wisconsin Archeological Society, and Midwestern Archaeology meetings, and have been gratified by the serious interest shown.

Tom Curtin and Don Rosso of Waveland Press saw the potential of case studies in critical thinking drawn from anthropology. Working with them is a rewarding experience.

Alice Beck Kehoe
Milwaukee, Wisconsin

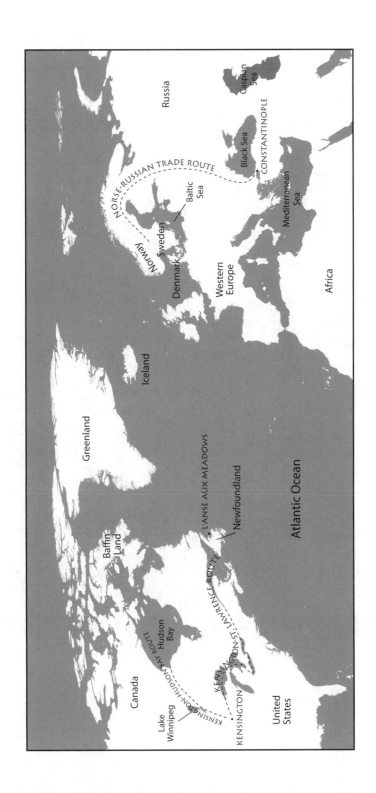

Introduction

Did an expedition of Norsemen reach northwestern Minnesota in 1362—more than a century before Columbus discovered America? Were ten of the men murdered there? Did their sorrowing comrades leave a monument in the form of a large stone?

The stone is a solid object that can be analyzed by geophysicists. Its engraved inscription, chiseled in the rune alphabet used in medieval Scandinavia, can be studied by experts on Norse languages and writing. Historians describe the technologies, politics, economics, and social values of medieval Scandinavia; we know that exporting furs was a critical source of income to the medieval Scandinavian kingdoms and that some of those furs came from what is now northeastern Canada. You would suppose that a team of experts armed with these scientific, literary, and historical data should be able to determine whether the stone, found by a farmer in 1898, is authentic or a hoax.

Several researchers have questioned the stone's authenticity, both back when it was found and now, a century later. In this book I explore the controversy surrounding the Kensington Runestone. Scientists considered it likely to be authentic, and historians were sure no White men penetrated America before well-known European colonizations. I am an anthropologist, accustomed to taking a holistic view encompassing data from archaeology, natural science, history, and human behavior. This led to recent researchers asking me to evaluate their data from an anthropologist's standpoint.

1

What I have seen is a fascinating struggle between "hard" scientists trained to dissect data and draw conclusions of probability, and historians hesitant to embrace a non-conforming interpretation.

I shall lay out the arguments on both sides of the controversy, tell something of the personalities involved and their backgrounds, and show how the claim that Norse reached Kensington, Minnesota, in 1362 ramifies through American history. My own background is neutral: I have no vested interest in Minnesota, and neither Scandinavian nor Italian ancestry. The controversy is intellectually stimulating, and that, by itself, makes it a provocative case for critical thinking.

Chapter One

Farmer Ohman's Find

The Kensington Runestone is a boulder $36'' \times 15'' \times 6''$, weighing 201 lb. 7 oz. The stone is a very hard metamorphosed rock called graywacke, originating in eastern Minnesota and carried by a continental glacier during the Pleistocene Ice Age to Kensington, in northwestern Minnesota. It came to light in September 1898, on a pioneer farm about twenty miles southwest of Alexandria, Minnesota. Swedish immigrant Olof Ohman, clearing a new field on his homestead, winched up some whole trees, roots and all. (The winch was donated to the Runestone Museum in Alexandria in 1959 by one of Olof's sons.) Ohman's ten-year-old son Edward came home from school and was sent out by his mother to bring his father an afternoon coffee. Hanging around his dad, Edward noticed a flat stone still held within the roots of one of the uprooted aspen stumps, used his cap to flick away clayey dirt on the stone, and saw what appeared to be carvings on its underside. When his son drew his attention to the strange marks, Ohman called over neighbor Nils Flaten, working nearby, to see the stone. Flaten had been there earlier, casually visiting, when Ohman cut the tree, one of many on the knoll; neither man saw anything unusual about the tree nor looked at the stone. The next day, Ohman chopped off the roots clasping the stone and hauled it and the stumps to the woodpile in his farmyard.

In the afternoon, Ohman went into town to shoemaker Hans Moen's shop. Moen was the village intellectual, actively interested in curiosities, who helped people understand legal documents. He went out to Ohman's farm in his horse and buggy with his own nine-year-old son. After examining the stone and the roots that had entwined it, Moen and his boy climbed into Ohman's wagon to ride out to examine the find spot. A number of other local people, including a traveling threshing crew, viewed the stone and roots in Ohman's yard during the next two weeks, after which it was put on display for two months in the window of the drugstore (or was it the bank, or, more likely, both?), in Kensington. John P. Hedberg, a real estate agent in Kensington, drew a copy of the inscription and mailed it to a Swedish-language newspaper published in Minneapolis. The editor, thinking it must be Greek, sent it to Greek-language scholars at the University of Minnesota, who recognized the letters as runes and passed the copy on to Olaus Breda, a Norwegian who taught Scandinavian languages at the university. Breda translated it except for the numbers, which he didn't know how to read. He told a campus newspaper in January 1899 that the words represent "a queer mixture of Swedish and Norwegian (Danish) and English words, the spelling of some words being such as to give the word a flavor of the old language." The inscription is likely a hoax, he concluded, although he suggested "the stone itself be critically examined" (Blegen 1968:20).

In late February 1899, the stone was shipped for evaluation to George Curme, professor of Old German at Northwestern University in Illinois. Curme examined it with an amateur geologist, John Steward, who photographed the stone and sent copies of the pictures to Scandinavian scholars. Curme hesitated to definitively confirm the authenticity of the inscription, although he noted that umlauts—pairs of dots over certain of the runes—were not used until the seventeenth century. The date carved on the stone could be read 1362. Admittedly, neither Breda nor Curme were scholarly experts in runes or medieval Norse. Also in late February, the Minneapolis Swedish-language newspaper published a sketch of the inscription, soon receiving translations from a couple of Minnesota readers. The stone was returned to Ohman, who put it in a grain shed on his farm. At the beginning of May, when the ground thawed, the County Superintendent of Schools from Alexandria brought eleven men to excavate at the find spot, but no artifacts or skeletons were discovered.

A decade later, in August 1907, a young historian named Hjalmar Holand stopped in at the Ohman farm. Holand was a graduate student at the University of Wisconsin who earned money during summers as a traveling salesman of books and maps. Starting in 1902, when the Norwegian Society was organized in Minneapolis to preserve information on Norwegian settlement in America, Holand served as its archivist, seeking out oral histories in pioneer communities. "It was slow but gratifying work because I was writing the saga of the Norwegian immigration to America" (Holand 1962:33). His preparation for the task was courses in history, Old Norse, and English literature at the University of Wisconsin, Madison. He mentions listening to the university's popular and famous professor of history, Frederick Jackson Turner, propounding his

> favorite theory [of] The Frontier as the Nursery of American Ideals. He insisted that American democracy was not the legacy of the early colonists who had come to seek liberty, but was born in the American forest, the product of the frontier. "The frontier," he wrote, "is the line of most rapid and effective Americanization." To me this was strange doctrine. I was at that time spending every summer on the frontier, gathering material for a history of the Norwegian immigration and a half-dozen other books on frontier life, and I found no signs of a rapid Americanization. The men whom I talked with on the edge of the wilderness had neither time nor knowledge to discuss abstract theories. They were too poor and too far away to have city newspapers and keep abreast of the national problems of the day. When they at infrequent intervals saw a distant neighbor, their conversation was . . . all in their native tongue. They had but one purpose and that was to conquer the wilderness and make it habitable. . . . European immigrants who made up three-fourths of the frontier population in the Middle West remained like foreign colonists in speech and manners for at least one generation. (Holand 1957:103)

Was it this experience of discovering how wrong an ivory-tower academic could be that propelled Holand to challenge academic dogma on the Kensington Runestone?

Holand's usual procedure was to visit towns in Minnesota and Wisconsin, go to pastors of Scandinavian churches to copy parish records, and ask around for "things of historical interest." Kensington, he found, "was started in 1867 . . . [by] a small group of Norwegians and Swedes . . . but as it was in a somewhat rough and swampy region, it did not prosper" (Holand 1962:33). The only "thing of historical interest" anyone there could think of was "a stone . . . with some writing on it." He was directed to Ohman's farm, where he interviewed Olof as a pioneer. Ohman stated that he had been born in 1855 in Hälsingland in northern Sweden, a forested region where he, like Nils Flaten from Norway, had become an expert in lumbering. In 1881, Ohman emigrated to northwestern Minnesota, worked as a farm laborer, and in 1891 "was able to buy a small tract of wild land where he settled" (Holand 1962:34).

When Ohman turned over the big flat stone in the shed and swept off its underside, Holand was amazed to see runes. "I had pondered over many runic inscriptions in my favorite study of Norse antiquities," he recalled, never expecting to see something of the sort in Minnesota. "Who could have inscribed it? . . . I asked Ohman for information about possibly learned persons with peculiar ideas, but he knew of none. 'I know them all,' he said, 'and they are all just plain people like myself'" (Holand 1962:34). In rural northern Sweden when Ohman was a boy, farm children received only six weeks of schooling per year, and he had, altogether, less than a year of formal schooling.

Holand explained to Ohman that he had studied runes in college and "wanted very much to study the inscription," in spite of its rejection by scholars eight years before. "After a little discussion, he gave me the stone," Holand reports, and it was shipped to Holand's home in Wisconsin (Holand 1962:35). It didn't take Holand long to decipher the inscription. Unlike Breda in 1899, Holand knew enough about runes to read the numerals, too. Holand wrote in disgust, "the conclusions of Professor Breda were without basis. He was unable to read the inscription, he disregarded the facts concerning the circumstance of the discovery, he ignored the weathering of the inscription, and without hesitation condemned the

The Kensington Runestone, shown lying flat on its back. Photo by Scott Wolter.

inscription as a fake and boasted of it. Was there ever such a pomp-
ous display of ignorance?" (Holand 1957:190).

On his way home from northern Minnesota, Holand spent time
in Minneapolis checking 1899 newspaper reports on the discovery.
A year later, in spring 1909, he returned to Kensington to check on
Ohman. Was he a skilled stonecutter? "Many times during the winter," Holand says, "I had admired the fine cutting of the runic
letters . . . which seemed to be the work of an artist with a cold-
chisel" (Holand 1962:36). But Mrs. Ohman told Holand that her
husband "is not a mason. He does some carpenter work when he has
time" (Holand 1962:37). The people of Kensington all spoke well of
Ohman as a respected citizen "who somehow managed to make a
living on a tract of land which all the early settlers had thought was
worthless" (Holand 1962:37). On this second visit, Mrs. Ohman
showed Holand the one book they had picturing runes, Almquist's
1840 *Svensk Språklära* (*Swedish Grammar*), a standard school
textbook. Holand noted that the example runic alphabet in the textbook did not show all the runes on the stone, and no numerals.

At this time, ten years after its discovery, Holand precipitated
a flurry of investigations of the Runestone. In 1908 the Norwegian
Society of Minneapolis appointed a three-man committee led by Dr.
Knut Hoegh, a medical doctor. Dr. Hoegh traveled to the Kensington area several times during that and the following year, joined by
Holand in 1909, and took formal notarized affidavits from Ohman,
Flaten, and two other Kensington men who had seen the stone,
roots, and find spot in 1898. Hoegh published his report in Norwegian in a magazine printed in Decorah, Iowa, for Norwegian-Americans. He affirmed the honesty and integrity of the Kensington men
and concluded that the Runestone was not likely a recent hoax. On
the other hand, Dr. Hoegh admitted he was neither a linguist nor a
geologist and could not evaluate the age of the carving nor the arguments that the runes and language were invalid.

These issues were addressed by two more committees, one
formed by the Minnesota Historical Society and the other by the
University of Illinois' Philological Society. The Illinois committee
consisted of three professors of English, two of German, a historian,
and the chair, George Flom, a professor of Scandinavian languages.
They met to examine a report and interpretation presented by Flom
after he heard Holand argue for the Runestone's authenticity to the
Chicago Historical Society in February 1910. Flom, like the other

Scandinavian-language linguists of his time, considered the inscription to reveal incompetencies in both Old Norse and runes, and therefore to be likely fraudulent. He went to Kensington, spoke with Ohman, and thought about the alleged 1362 event: Would men who had just come upon their comrades "red with blood and dead" "coolly sit down and remain"—sitting ducks for renewed massacre—while the artisan in their party so precisely and neatly chiseled such a long narrative on the hard rock? (Blegen 1968:65). Flom's colleagues at Illinois endorsed his negative conclusion.

In contrast, the Minnesota Historical Society committee espoused the ideas recommended by Dr. Hoegh. Led by Minnesota's eminent state geologist, Newton Winchell, it included another geologist, Warren Upham, who was the Historical Society's librarian; a man who had served on Major John Wesley Powell's exploration of the Colorado River; an amateur archaeologist; and a scholar of early Christianity. None of the committee members was competent in Norse linguistics or runes, so they wrote to academics in these fields for opinions. Winchell and Upham, by virtue of their training and experience, were most concerned with the physical aspects of the stone and its find spot. Winchell's investigation and notes are described in the chapter on geological tests of the Runestone in this book.

Winchell, the most active member of the Minnesota Historical Society committee, made three trips to Kensington, examining the find site, noting the scatter of similar glacier-carried boulders in the area, and interviewing Ohman, his neighbors, and townspeople. He listened to Holand's reading of the inscription and argument for authenticity. Regardless of whether Holand's opinion, at odds with the pronouncements of all the better-known scholars, carried much weight with Winchell, it did fit his evaluation as determined through his considerable experience as a Minnesota geologist. The Minnesota committee concluded in spring 1910, "That this Committee regards the genuineness of the supposed Kensington Rune Stone as not established, but that they deem the preponderance of evidence to be in favor of the Stone" (quoted in Blegen 1968:89). Then in July 1910, the committee met again to discuss George Flom's paper and decided to retract the statement. The Minnesota Historical Society's Executive Council "reserve their conclusion until more agreement of opinions for or against the runic inscription may be attained"—this final statement was printed in their *Preliminary Report* in 1915 (quoted in Blegen 1968:91).

Warren Upham, on behalf of the Historical Society's Committee, requested opinions from four Scandinavian scholars, mailing each photographs of the inscription (rather than copies on paper, which might be attacked as inaccurate). Holand planned to take the stone itself to Scandinavia, and the committee considered having Winchell go with Holand. He did not, nor did the committee arrange for European geologists to examine weathering of the runes and the stone as a whole. Authenticity would rest upon the linguistic issues.

At that, Holand asked the Minnesota Historical Society for a stipend to pay for the trip to Europe with the stone. There is controversy over whether Holand was really selling the stone for $2500— or $3000 stipend plus $2000 for the stone—because Holand said that if he received the stipend, he would give legal title to the stone to the Minnesota Historical Society. But it seems that Ohman meant to *lend* the stone to Holand for study, and later decided it should be kept in St. Paul in the State Capitol building. The Minnesota Historical Society sent a representative out to Kensington to execute a proper legal document, paying Ohman ten dollars on April 19, 1911. Ninety dollars more was to be appropriated by the Society to complete the purchase of the stone. Three weeks later, the Society's Executive Council met and voted against such appropriation, voting instead to give the stone back to Holand without any stipend for further study. Ohman was informed of the decision and was apparently allowed to keep the ten dollars, but the bill of sale he had signed was not returned to him. The stone remained in Minnesota except for its European forays, a year on exhibit at the Smithsonian Institution in Washington, D.C. in February 1948– February 1949, and a showing at the 1965 World's Fair in New York City. In 1957 it had returned to northwestern Minnesota, to be displayed in the museum built for it at the county seat, Alexandria.

Holand and the Runestone arrived in Europe through a 1911 celebration of the Norse conquest of Normandy in Rouen, France. His expenses for Rouen covered, Holand committed to sending weekly articles to *Skandinaven*, the Norwegian-language newspaper published in Chicago and St. Paul, and collected donations from Chicago friends. Many noted scholars assembled at Rouen for a two-week history conference. Holand gave his paper on the Runestone (in English, with a French translator beside him). Oscar Montelius, a Swede and one of the greatest archaeologists of the time, heard him and when he finished, stood up—over six feet tall and broad-shouldered—to bring up certain objections. Young Hjalmar from Wisconsin held his ground before the distinguished professor:

> I was familiar with the points he raised, so I was able to make a tolerable answer, and we tossed the ball back and forth for a few minutes. Finally Montelius was gracious enough to admit that his objections were dispelled, wished me good luck, and said he would be glad to help me when I came to Sweden. (Holand 1957:199)

On the last day of the conference, all the presenters gathered for a formal group portrait, and on a sturdy chair, draped with an American flag, centered in front of the president of the conference was the Runestone itself.

From Rouen, Holand went on to Denmark by way of Paris, Cologne, and Berlin, which in his patriotic estimation was "an inferior replica of Chicago" (Holand 1957:206). Maybe he was jaundiced by suffering prolonged lack of good Scandinavian-style coffee with cream—French and German cups served with skim milk couldn't satisfy him. What a relief to reach Denmark and a train-station stall with just the coffee he loved! Copenhagen's Royal (National) Museum impressed him with its wealth of handsome Bronze Age artifacts. Stockholm's museum was next, enhanced by a personal tour by Montelius, its director. Journey's end was Oslo, where the Runestone was exhibited as Holand lectured on it. There, and in Uppsala, Lund, and Copenhagen, Holand consulted university libraries and eminent philologists on medieval Norse languages. Holand made a second trip to Europe in 1928, before publishing his book *The Kensington Stone: A Study in Pre-Columbian American History* in 1932. His last research trip took place in 1950 thanks to a prestigious Guggenheim Foundation fellowship (he notes the application form specified it was limited to persons under the age of 40, and he was 78, but figures the Guggenheim committee paid attention only to letters of recommendation) (Holand 1957:253). This last trip focused on medieval architecture, searching for similarities to the Newport Tower brought to his attention by Philip Ainsworth Means, who had died in 1942. Holand did find prototypes in Cistercian abbeys and Swedish round churches. He interpreted the Newport Tower as further evidence for a Norse expedition to America in 1355–1364; an expedition alluded to, he believed, in the Kensington Stone.

Chapter Two

The Controversy

On the face of it, the debate over whether the Kensington Rune-stone is a hoax pits linguists who found errors in the runes and language against people convinced that the farmer Ohman and his associates would not, or could not, perpetuate such a hoax. The Minnesota Historical Society decided in 1910 that they needed evaluations of the inscription by the best authorities on medieval Scandinavian linguistics. The Society's secretary, Warren Upham, asked Olaus Breda, former professor at the University of Minnesota and then living in Norway. Breda replied that he thought "an utter absurdity" the idea of such a carving having been cut by fourteenth-century Norse deep in interior America. But as requested, he listed Scandinavian authorities who, he claimed, "unanimously pronounced the Kensington inscription a fraud and a forgery of recent date": Sophus Bugge, Adolf Noreen, Magnus Olsen, Oluf Rygh, and Gustav Storm. Upham added to this list Gisle Bothne, who had taken Breda's position in Minnesota, George Curme of Northwestern University, Starr Cutting and Chester Gould of the University of Chicago, George Flom of the University of Illinois, Rasmus Anderson and Julius Olson (Holand's teacher) of the University of Wisconsin, and Helge Gjessing in Norway (Blegen 1968:86–88). Only Hjalmar Holand, dismissed as an avocational historian, insisted the inscription should be taken as vernacular language and runes from a period before writing was standardized.

In spite of such an impressive roster of nay-saying authorities, the Runestone would not go down. Theodore Blegen, both a head of the Minnesota Historical Society and dean of the University of Minnesota Graduate School, marshaled the Historical Society's voluminous archives to detail the circumstances of the 1898 discovery and ensuing investigations. His 1968 book intended to lay speculation to rest: "The sum total of historical, runological, and archaeological evidence . . . is, in my judgment, conclusive. The inscription is a fake" (Blegen 1968:123). Olof Ohman, he suspected, was the hoaxer. The stone's indefatigable champion, Hjalmar Holand, had died five years earlier, in 1963. Who would be so foolish as to carry on the fight in defiance of the scholar called "Mr. Minnesota History"?

"Ave Maria fræelse af illum" says the stone, "Hail Mary deliver us from evils." Whatever the linguists declared, there remained the unwavering insistence of Kensington folk that Olof Ohman and Nils Flaten were honest men. And there is the stone itself, those grayed runes contrasting with the sparkling white of the "H" Holand carved into a lower corner already almost a century ago. Newton Winchell was an eminent authority in his field of geology, Minnesota State Archaeologist, and professor of geology and mineralogy at the University of Minnesota (its geology building is named after him). Both he and Warren Upham directed archaeology for the Minnesota Historical Society in the early 1900s. Winchell wrote to Holand in April 1911, "You must understand that . . . I personally think the stone is valid and vindicated" (quoted in Wahlgren 1958:102).

Are opinions of linguists more compelling than opinions of geologists? Should the literally hard science of mineralogy, carried out in field and laboratory, be given less weight than the opinions of scholars of language? What about compilations of runes from fourteenth-century manuscripts? In the 1980s, Richard Nielsen, a Danish-American engineer with a doctorate in materials science, became interested in the Kensington Runestone. His background inclined him to respect Winchell's conclusion. The question, to Nielsen, was: How sound is the data base on which the linguists depended? Are there fourteenth-century runic manuscripts not known, or not consulted by, the linguists who studied the stone? Nielsen's work gave him opportunities to delve into Scandinavian and German manuscript archives. He began to find some of the supposedly erroneous runes and words in unassailable medieval manuscripts. He also was told by a professor of medieval Norse whom he consulted that the Runestone's variants from standard Old Norse look like the dialect spoken in the Swedish province of Bohuslän. Had Olaus Breda and his peers been familiar with the fourteenth-century Bohuslän dialect? Nielsen felt he had reason to doubt.

Olof Ohman (left) and Hjalmar Holand (right), 1927.
Photo from Runestone Museum.

It happened that in 1990, vacationers Barry and Alice Hanson stopped in Alexandria, Minnesota and looked at the Runestone in the local museum. Hanson, like Nielsen, is trained in science and managed engineering projects. He wondered whether a poor immigrant Swedish farmer would be so dishonest as to carve an elaborate hoax and then steadfastly insist it was an inadvertent find. Hanson thought of his own immigrant grandparents, how concerned they were that their integrity and work ethic would be above reproach. It seemed to Hanson that we owed farmer Ohman an opportunity to check on his story by conducting mineralogical tests on the Runestone in one of today's high-tech labs. A scanning electron microscope ought to give us data on weathering on the stone relevant to the issue of the age of the inscription.

Hanson surfed the Internet and soon hit on Richard Nielsen's work. Nielsen agreed that testing the carvings with contemporary high-tech equipment would be sensible. The two men found a geophysics laboratory in St. Paul capable of supervising the tests. Its proprietor, Scott Wolter, had never heard of the Kensington Runestone but quickly became interested in the scientific problem. Nielsen and Hanson then had to persuade the board of directors of the Runestone Museum in Alexandria to let the stone travel to the lab and to have a small sample be removed. Understandably, they hesitated to revive the controversy. Then, the Smithsonian Institution asked to borrow the Runestone to display in an upcoming blockbuster show on "The Vikings." Beside the stone would be a label informing the public that it is a hoax. Nielsen and Hanson convinced the Runestone Museum that this would be unfair. The Smithsonian's curator, William Fitzhugh, politely stood firm on the label. Reluctantly, the Runestone Museum directors agreed to let Nielsen and Hanson arrange to have the stone scanned and sampled, and refused to send it to Washington to be scorned.

I came into the picture because I am one of the few American archaeologists who think it unlikely that the Americas were wholly isolated from the rest of the world until 1492. Although a good deal of what is put forward as evidence of pre-Colombian contacts is ill-informed, a good scientist should not automatically assume all non-professionals are fools. My willingness to listen brought me into acquaintance with Nielsen, and when he and Hanson launched their Runestone project, I agreed to advise them on archaeological aspects. I arranged for them and Wolter to present their evidence to

a joint meeting of the Plains Anthropological and Midwest Archaeological Conferences in St. Paul in 2000, where the Runestone itself
stood in the front of the room, trucked over from Wolter's nearby
lab. Along with the laboratory work, all three men, Nielsen, Hanson, and Wolter, have delved deeply into the Minnesota Historical
Society archives and libraries to read firsthand the pros and cons
put out a century ago. By 2003, they wanted to present their data
to the staff of the Minnesota Historical Society.

Guy Gibbon, professor of anthropology at the University of
Minnesota, introduced the 2003 symposium on the Runestone with
a simple chart like a thermometer: Where, on a scale from "proven"
to "disproven," does the weight of data lie? What is the *probability*
that the Runestone is authentic? Perhaps a better model of the
issue would be a scale—loading pro data on one pan and con data
on the other, which way does it tip? As archaeologists, Gibbon and
I have seen many fakes. The Runestone doesn't look obviously fake
to us, and unlike most offerings of fakes, no one tried to make
money from it. Holand had asked the Minnesota Historical Society
for compensation for time and travel he had already put in and for
research support. Scoffers claim that Ohman perpetuated the hoax
maliciously or as a prank, or that Holand and other Norwegian-
Americans wanted to glorify their forebears. These are supposi-
tions. Gibbon and I, looking on as anthropologists familiar with philosophy of science (Gibbon 1989, Kehoe 1998), see, on the one hand,
the inertia of mainstream science—the Runestone is a hoax, "every-
body knows that"—and on the other hand, anomalies that press
upon the accepted position. The range of data and interpretations,
from geophysics to world history, calls for the anthropological perspective, weaving together hard science and humanities.

History is a discipline relevant to the Kensington Runestone.
Olaus Breda's quick denunciation of the inscription, repeated in his
reply to Upham's 1910 committee, quashed any interest by professional historians. No one has brought up the unique circumstances
of the early 1360s in Scandinavia that weigh toward probability on
the scale. The Black Death hit Scandinavia in 1351, killing—depend-
ing on the region—from one-third to one-half its inhabitants. The
German merchants' Hanseatic League muscled in, taking over Scandinavia's principal port, Bergen, and its lucrative transshipment of
Russian furs in 1360. Sweden's king had lost most of his territory in
war with Denmark and had been deposed from ruling Norway.

Norse had been living in Greenland for nearly four centuries, crossing over to Canada for building timber and furs. Driven by the Hanseatic takeover to search for new sources for export furs, a party of Scandinavians may well have pushed inland far past their Greenlandic cousins' Atlantic habitat. If they managed to return home, they would have been called up for the fight against the Hansa being mounted by the newly allied three Scandinavian kingdoms.

Unfortunately for his efforts on behalf of the Runestone, Holand argued that the inscription could only be accounted for by a commission given by King Magnus of Sweden to the nobleman Paul Knutson (Pál Knutsson) in 1354. The king had been informed that the western Norse settlement in Greenland had been abandoned in the 1340s. He wanted Knutson to check, emphasizing that Christian communities had been established in this far western land, and the king, as guardian of the faith, wished to ensure it would continue there. It is surely pertinent that in 1348, Magnus had invaded Finland and that the Black Death the next year forced Magnus to give up what he was waging as a crusade against infidels. In 1351 the Pope urged him to resume this enterprise, financed with a loan from the Vatican. Again Magnus gave it up, now with the Pope demanding repayment of the loan and Magnus without the economic gain he had hoped from conquering northern Russia. Magnus didn't have money—might the Pope forgive the loan if Magnus ostentatiously sent a nobleman to recover apostate Christians on the other side of the world? The gesture was futile: the Pope excommunicated Magnus in 1355. No record seems to exist of whether Knutson did carry out his king's commission. If he did, there is no reason to think he would have gone on more than a thousand miles past Greenland. Holand characterizing the Knutson commission as a "crusade" driven by religious fervor left him vulnerable to skeptics denouncing the flimsy Knutson story and, by implication, the Runestone inscription.

By insisting that the inscription recorded a 1350s *non-commercial* venture (Holand 1962:26), Holand deflected attention from historical circumstances in Scandinavia in 1361. Looking from those circumstances, it is reasonable that a party of Swedish Götlanders and Norwegians pushed inland so far beyond the Greenlanders' accustomed hunting and trading locales. The trip would have been a westward version of the eastern trading route Scandinavians used for centuries, through the far northern forests and marshes of present-day Russia to the headwaters of the Volga, down it for two thousand miles to the Caspian Sea and thence to the fabled metropolis of Constantinople (now Istanbul)—and back again. When a man died on one of these lengthy journeys, his comrades might erect a memorial stone to him home in Sweden, inscribing it in runes; the custom had more or less died out by 1360 but thousands of standing stones kept it familiar to Scandinavians.

Would the Kensington Runestone be accepted as valid if Holand hadn't crusaded for his Knutson Crusade story? Probably not. Every schoolchild knows that "in 1492, Columbus sailed the ocean blue," launching American history. Leif Ericson's colony in "Vinland" gets mentioned as a premature attempt to settle in America. After a flurry of explorations around 1500, jump to 1607 and the English establishment at Jamestown in Virginia. Then English royalty sets up the Hudson's Bay Company in 1670, linking America into European commerce via the fur trade. Textbook histories have been Anglo history, passing over sixteenth-century Spanish and French colonizations and potent repercussions on balances of power among America's First Nations. To put Norsemen in Minnesota in 1362 means rewriting American history, including "prehistory."

An anthropological perspective sees the standard narrative of American history to be more than simplification. It functions as a myth. This is not to say it's fantasy. In the 1920s, anthropologist Bronislaw Malinowski recorded and analyzed myths told in communities in the Trobriand Islands off New Guinea. Malinowski had a radical approach to his work—instead of, as he put it, sitting on a veranda formally interviewing elders of a tribe, he got down and dirty, pitching a tent on the edge of a village and engaging in everyday activities. A couple of years of such participant observation, interrupted by a year back home analyzing his notes, gave the fieldworker insights not only into Trobriand society but into our own. He heard histories of how ruling families had gained their office; intriguingly, one community's heroine was a rival town's bad guy. Malinowski realized that each town's legendary history—myth—legitimated its present status and relationships. It was, he said, a "social charter" setting out the proper officers and structure, business, and responsibilities of the society, much like the charter of a corporation. Should the economics of the society change, its chartering myth would change, too. Today we could call this spin doctoring.

The United States was originally thirteen British colonies. Its chartering history therefore tells its English beginning at Jamestown and soon after at Plymouth, begetting a line of English plantations and towns coalescing into the thirteen colonies. American First Nations come in only in the persons of Powhatan, Pocahontas, and Squanto, enablers through whom the English people survived. The failed 1587 Roanoke English colony gets mentioned but not the failed 1571 Spanish Jesuit mission in Chesapeake Bay closer to Jamestown (although the Indian leader who killed the priests had spent ten years in Cuba, visited Spain, and must have told the Powhatan about Europeans). A series of personages and events in standard school-books charter elements in American society: George Washington, the ideal brave, steadfast, and wise father, legitimating the presidency; Lincoln suffering civil war, martyred as Martin Luther King, Jr. would be a century later to resurrect and heal our people's unity; Teddy Roosevelt championing conservation; Franklin Roosevelt, with the half-American Winston Churchill, saving humanity from Hitler's satanic madness. Schoolbooks deliberately instill pride and love for our country as it came to be, English-speaking, relatively democratic, literate, capitalist. Particularly during the nineteenth and early twentieth centuries, as the United States expanded from sea to sea and beyond, its dominant English and Scots culture asserted superiority to every conquered First Nation, Spanish, and non-Anglo immigrant culture. The power of the dominant class was legitimated, was chartered, through the history it taught.

Up until the National Geographic Society announcement of the 1960s discovery of a medieval Norse settlement in Newfoundland, many historians considered descriptions of "Vinland" in Icelandic sagas to be myths. The sagas mentioning Vinland were written down more than two centuries after the events, and exactly where and how big Vinland was is not recorded. Helge Ingstad, a Norwegian mariner, deduced the northern tip of Newfoundland to fit sailing routes in the sagas, and with his archaeologist wife Anne Stine Ingstad, tested and excavated a site on a cove, L'Anse aux Meadows. Foundations of a rectangular timber hall, slag from smelted bog iron, and artifacts including a Norse-style spindle weight resembled Scandinavian and Greenlandic Norse village sites, and radiocarbon dating techniques dated the remains at approximately A.D. 1000, when the sagas said Eric the Red's adult children attempted to colonize "Vinland" west of Greenland.

Logically, confirmation of Norse settlement at the Strait of Belle Isle leading into the Gulf of St. Lawrence should have positively weighted the probability of Norse elsewhere in northeastern America. Norse could even have accessed the interior via the St. Lawrence River and Great Lakes, or through Hudson's Bay. Instead, most archaeologists and historians insist medieval Norse only crossed Davis Strait between Greenland and Canada's Labrador, and barely entered the Gulf of St. Lawrence stretching south beyond Newfoundland.

According to the Icelandic sagas, Norse in Vinland traded with native people and battled them. Most historians suppose the Norse decided it was too dangerous to settle in Vinland. The Kensington Runestone's memorial to ten men "red with blood and dead" seemed to confirm danger that would keep Norse out of America. Yet European history and Icelandic sagas picture Norsemen, and Norsewomen, too, to be intrepid fighters; their regular trade journeys across the length of Russia were highly dangerous. Norse armed with crossbows, swords, and battle-axes quickly abandoning Canada's Maritimes seems out of character. Perhaps American historians have been influenced, unconsciously, by the legitimating myth that America was a wilderness populated by merciless savages until Christian Europeans transformed it. Thomas Jefferson, who knew better, used the myth to justify rebellion: King George, he claimed as a "Fact" (his word), "has endeavoured to bring on the inhabitants of our frontiers, the merciless Indian Savages, whose known rule of warfare, is an undistinguished destruction, of all ages, sexes and conditions" (Declaration of Independence, 1776). Those "merciless Indian Savages" on Virginia's frontiers were later called the Five Civilized Tribes, farmers and plantation owners defending their homes against Virginia land speculators. Jefferson could get away with his inflammatory rhetoric because it was a convention for English conquerors—first the Irish were called "savages," then the American peoples. John Locke, employed in the 1690s by English aristocrats planning to exploit American lands, wrote well-received philosophical treatises claiming America represented the crude beginnings of human culture, her peoples so primitive that they had no right to property. America as the Land of Savages was a chartering myth. It not only legitimated the United States' and Canada's conquests, it conveniently could be invoked to explain why Norse never gained a foothold on the continent.

With this overview of the controversy about Norse in America generally and the Kensington Runestone in particular, we can examine aspects of the controversy in more detail using hard evidence from geology, linguistics, historical circumstances in 1362, and the significance the Runestone could have for American history. That tough slab of graywacke with rows of neatly chiseled runes is an anomaly, not what one would expect in a forgery, and not what history books narrate. Anomalies play a critical role in science, pushing researchers to refine or reject theories. How do data from twenty-first-century laboratories and more than a hundred years of additional research into medieval Norse languages and writing affect opinions voiced by the Runestone's first debaters?

Chapter Three

What Can
Archaeology Show?

Why not dig at the site where the Runestone was found? Wouldn't that show whether Norsemen had been there? Yes, if there had been occupation of the site for long enough to accumulate garbage and man-made changes in the land surface. Not likely, if it had been only a briefly used campsite. Remains from a brief camp might be so few and scattered that excavating sections of the knoll would likely not uncover those few artifacts or disturbances. In other words, archaeology has positive results if evidence of human activity is encountered, but if nothing is encountered it should be interpreted as unproven rather than definitively disproven. Lacking positive finds, archaeological investigation is inconclusive, although the weight of probability may be shifted down.

The first excavation at the Runestone site took place in early May after the 1898 discovery, after the ground had thawed. Eleven local men led by the county superintendent of schools dug on the knoll where the aspen tree had grown. Four feet down they came upon "some fragments 4 to 5 inches in length which resembled limestone but were thought to have great likeness to moldered bones" (letter by Olaus Olson, May 16, 1899, to *Svenska Amerikanska Posten* newspaper, quoted in Blegen 1968:135). The fragments are not mentioned again.

The Minnesota Historical Society sponsored a professional archaeological investigation in 1964. Trenches totaling over 300 feet were excavated where Olof Ohman's son Arthur thought the stone had been found, as well as higher on the knoll where a 1910 photograph showed Ohman, Flaten, and another man standing beside an American flag. "Nothing of significance was found," Blegen states (1968:136). The archaeologist recommended broader excavation before he could be confident he had been working exactly where the Runestone had been discovered; the find spot might show only that a tree had been uprooted, something not in doubt.

If the Runestone had been standing upright for many years and had attracted attention from Indians traveling or living nearby, they might have placed offerings such as tobacco, ornaments, arrows, or pots of food beside it to win the good will of whatever spirit could be invoked by the strange symbols. Linea Sundstrom, an archaeologist familiar with Lakota and Dakota rock art and shrines, suggests (personal communication, 2004) that ornaments, arrowpoints, and pottery left at rock shrines often remain visible. If nothing of this sort was noticed, we may hypothesize that the stone, if standing for long, was obscured by trees, or perhaps fell (or was pushed over by animals rubbing against it) before many decades had passed. At any rate, there is no evidence it had any significance to Indian people.

In 1981, a Minnesota Historical Society Archaeological Survey crew led by Christina Harrison systematically checked known pre-colonization sites in the county where the Runestone was found. They located dozens more stones, none of them large or unusual. This crew investigated boulders with holes said to be chiseled out by Norse to hold iron spikes to which boats could be moored; they interviewed a neighbor to the Ohman farm who vividly remembered his father and others making such holes for blasting powder to break up rocks on their homesteads. In 2001, another archaeologist, Michael Michlovic, joined Harrison to test another knoll north of the Runestone's find spot (now called Runestone Hill), where what turned out to be a real hoax had been noticed. That stone had been carved with the letters AVM and the date 1363 by student pranksters in 1985; two confessed after publicity on the "new runestone" in 2001. Instead of trenches, the 2001 archaeologists used a method common today called shovel probes: every ten meters along a transect line, they dug a quarter-meter-square hole down to sandy loam subsoil, about a half-meter deep. Once more, no positive indications of Norse. While Michlovic and Harrison probed along their transects, geologist Scott Wolter used a metal detector on the area. Wolter dug where his instrument indicated metal and found bits of barbed wire and a shotgun shell, all unquestionably historic. The archaeologists found a few pieces of chipped stone and broken animal bone, very likely prehistoric but not diagnostic of any ethnic group or time period.

L'ANSE AUX MEADOWS

To appreciate the difficulty of applying archaeology to the Kensington Runestone site, let us look at its opposite, the American site where archaeology conclusively demonstrated medieval Norse occupation. Note that "conclusively demonstrated" is about as close to "proved" as archaeology can go. A sharp trial lawyer could still jab at the evidence: Couldn't an unidentified American Indian culture have built turf-covered longhouses? Couldn't the one spindle weight and the one bronze pin have been dropped by a sixteenth-century explorer or seventeenth-century colonist? Likewise, could the smelted bog iron be from the seventeenth century? The weight of probability may all lie on the side of Norse occupation, but that's not the same as written documentation by reliable witnesses.

Helge Ingstad was a Norwegian mariner who spent many years studying maps, historical records, Icelandic sagas, and the North Atlantic ocean. He collated and analyzed this great variety of information to sift possibly valid data from secondhand copying and distorted legends. Ingstad's work was long-term, systematic, and physically adventurous, sailing in a small boat past looming icebergs and towering rocky cliffs. Helge's wife, Anne Stine Ingstad, was a trained archaeologist. The couple sailed in 1953 along the western coast of Greenland, going ashore to examine the ruins of its medieval Norse farms and churches, as well as visiting archaeological excavations in southeastern Greenland and Iceland. The couple thus gained familiarity not only with the appearance of traces of buried structures, but also with the landscapes favored by those Norse.

Too far north to grow cereal crops, Greenlandic Norse depended on grazing livestock for milk, meat, and wool, supplemented by hunted caribou, seals, other game, and fish. Helge Ingstad knew that the word *vin* commonly was prefixed to Norwegian place-names denoting good pastures. Therefore, he reasoned that the name "Vinland" in Icelandic sagas meant a place of good pasture (not wine grapes, as some scholars had supposed). Carefully compounding remarks in the sagas about sailing times and directions, Ingstad derived the most probable route for Norse from settlements in Greenland west to mainland North America and hypothesized that Norse settlements in America, described in three Icelandic saga histories, would have been located at good pastures near the coast.

In 1960, Helge Ingstad traveled by boat and air around Newfoundland looking for likely locations for a Norse "Vinland." At the island's northern tip he saw wide green pastures around a cove with a little fishing village called L'Anse aux Meadows. Three earlier researchers had deduced the area as a likely site, but had not located the ruins. One of the village fishermen, primed to recognize sod-house remains by a 1956 survey by a Danish archaeologist, took Ingstad to a brook coursing through a meadow with low grassy house-sized mounds. The site fit the landscape selected by Norse in Greenland and Iceland, and the low mounds resembled Norse ruins there. The next summer, 1961, the Ingstads reconnoitered the Canadian Maritimes. They began in Montreal and sailed down the St. Lawrence River to its mouth in the Gulf of St. Lawrence and then along Quebec and Labrador to the Strait of Belle Isle and Newfoundland. For the next seven years, Helge and Anne Stine Ingstad, assisted by small crews of experienced archaeologists from Iceland, Sweden, Norway, Canada, and the United States, excavated the site at Épaves Bay near the village of L'Anse aux Meadows. In contrast to the Minnesota knoll where the Kensington Runestone was found, the L'Anse aux Meadows site was obviously particularly suited for habitation and had quite visible remnants of structures. No shovel probes along arbitrary transect lines in hopes of chancing upon artifacts—the Ingstads could see their targets and lay out excavations to expose the buried remains.

The archaeologists opened one-meter square test spots, dug slowly and sensitively with sharpened trowels, placed artifacts—everything made by people—and charcoal in bags labeled with the exact find spot, and made photographs and scale drawings before anything exposed was disturbed. All these procedures are standard in archaeology. That first year, nothing typical of American Indian occupations appeared, nor did anything distinctively Norse. The Ingstads decided to continue exploring the Labrador coast, and Anne Stine returned to Épaves Bay at the end of summer for more testing. This time, she trenched where a few stones were visible, as no stones occurred naturally on this seaside meadow. It turned out that the few stones were not a house foundation, but her trenches revealed faint outlines of blocks of turf such as found in Norse house sites in Greenland that utilized such blocks to make buildings. She also found rusted iron rivets that looked like medieval Norse rivets, and remnants of hearths that were Norse, not American Indian, in style. Anne Stine checked a report on archaeology at a farmstead in Greenland built by Eirik the Red, leader of Norse colonization there (A.D. 986), as well as that of his son Leif, who is said to have tried to colonize Vinland. The hearth closely resembled hearths in Eiriksson's house. The Épaves Bay site warranted more extensive investigation.

The Norwegian Research Council for Science and the Humanities and the (U.S.) National Geographic Society agreed to sponsor the Ingstads' work, with additional contributions from many scientific institutions and interested Norwegians. The international teams working at the site between 1962 and 1968 included men and women whose scientific skills and archaeological experience highly qualified them for the project, and other experts were brought in for consultation. The seven long seasons proceeded with care to meet every question thoroughly, openly, and with wide discussion. The dig was often physically daunting:

> Not only did the excavation of the remains of ancient turf houses with vague and diffuse features present many difficulties, but the climate at its worst, when cold winds, fog or rain come in from the Labrador Sea, can be downright abominable. It is hard for anyone to spend any length of time excavating under such conditions. (Ingstad 1977:16)

Quite a different picture of archaeology from Indiana Jones in a tropical paradise!

By the conclusion of the seven-year project, L'Anse aux Meadows had yielded eight, perhaps nine, collapsed turf-block houses typical of those found on Iceland farmsteads from around A.D. 1000; four boat sheds near the water, another typical Norse structure; a probable bath-house; a smithy with an anvil stone and iron slag from local bog-iron deposits; a charcoal kiln; a bronze pin with a ring through an eye; a bronze belt-buckle prong; fragments of red jasper from Iceland, used with an iron firesteel, also found, to strike sparks to make fire; two fragments of domestic animal bone, probably pig; a Norse-style bone knitting needle and stone needle sharpeners; iron rivets and a smelted copper fragment (American-Indian-made copper items were not smelted); a simple stone lamp that the Ingstads thought looked Icelandic; and a soapstone spindle weight (whorl) of standard Scandinavian type. The team also found a couple of stone arrowheads of Dorset Eskimo type along with chert flakes, an ax, a scraper, and a blade that could have been Dorset in a sheltered area with a large shallow pit used for cooking. These may represent Dorset Eskimo people camping at the village after the Norse had abandoned it.

This brings us to a question raised by both radiocarbon dates and shallow occupation layers from L'Anse aux Meadows. Evidence indicates the houses were built right around A.D. 1000 and not rebuilt, although turf-block structures don't last more than about thirty years. Four boat sheds suggest four boats with four crews or families plus servants and laborers—perhaps thirty or forty people. Why did they leave after a few years? The climate and pasture were good for cows, sheep, and pigs; iron ore was available, as were forests of timber for building and fuel and seals, salmon, cod, and caribou for food—everything a Greenlandic or Icelandic Norse family would want. The Ingstads premise that the settlers may have feared attacks from Eskimos or Indians, which could have come by sea in canoes or over the ridge backing the bay. Perhaps native people killed grazing livestock for easy game. However, no evidence of violence was found, suggesting the village was deliberately abandoned. Norse lived in Greenland for five more centuries, but never returned to L'Anse aux Meadows.

Parks Canada took over the site, employing archaeologists to conduct three more seasons of fieldwork during 1973–1976 directed by Birgitta Lineroth Wallace, a Swedish-born archaeologist who had worked on the Ingstads' project. Her work uncovered butternut shells, highly significant because butternut trees never grew so far north; the shells indicate Norse sailed to the southern portion of the Gulf of St. Lawrence, perhaps into the mouth of the St. Lawrence River. Knowledge of warmer-latitude resources and this major river from the west would have been as valuable as the nuts and perhaps other foods and timber. After its archaeological investigations, Parks Canada constructed replicas of houses and a museum. L'Anse aux Meadows Norse Settlement is now open to tourists.

ARCHAEOLOGICAL EVIDENCE FOR
NORSE AND ENGLISH IN ARCTIC CANADA

Scattered finds of small items of Norse origin are reported by archaeologists excavating in Arctic Canada. Most wonderful is a wooden carving of a person in a long hooded robe split in front, with a cross on the chest. Surely it represents a Norseman, possibly a priest or a knight who joined one of the crusader orders. (Helge Ingstad remarks that the long robe was impractical for sailors or hunters [Ingstad 2001:176].) The little figurine lay in a winter house of thirteenth-century Thule Eskimo type on the north shore of Hudson Strait, and the style of carving is Thule, not European or Greenlandic Norse. Fragments of European smelted iron and copper, a piece of chain mail, a strip of woolen cloth, and a portion of a bronze weighing-scale pan came out of Inuit Eskimo sites from the Canadian High Arctic. The Thule, forebears of historic Inuit, used metal tools centuries before European colonization, manufacturing iron knives from iron meteors in the eastern Arctic. Meteoric iron is pure, not requiring smelting as mined ore does, so metal fragments indicating smelting originated outside Thule territory.

A penny coin minted in Norway between 1065 and 1080 was excavated in a site on the Maine coast. Everything else in the site is American Indian, with radiocarbon dates about a century later than the coin. Stone artifacts include some made from top-quality material widely traded from outcrops in Labrador and Nova Scotia. Thus, the Norwegian coin may have traveled down the Atlantic coast from the region visited by Greenlandic Norse for timber. Its value as a shiny ornament was much greater than its monetary value back in Norway.

Confusion exists over rock-built longhouses in several regions of the eastern Canadian Arctic. These have no evidence of roofs, and may have had a row of tents inside, somewhat protected from strong winds by the stone walls; possibly they were roofed with overturned boats. They are different from Norse long halls such as seen at L'Anse aux Meadows, Greenland, and Iceland. Similarly, stone cairns are common in the Arctic, erected by Inuit to deflect caribou toward hunters. There are no inscriptions on Inuit cairns. A rune-stone has been recovered from Kingiktorsuag in northern Greenland; it reads, "Erling Sigvatsson, Bjarne Tordsson and Eindride

Oddsson erected these cairns on Saturday before Rogation Day, and
runed well" (Ingstad 2001:172). Three stone cairns, more neatly
built than Inuit hunting devices, stand by the runestone. Its date is
believed to be 1333. A number of Norse items occur along with Inuit
artifacts in this region of northern Greenland where medieval
Norse hunted. Furs, walrus-tusk ivory and hides, and white falcons
were taken by Norse, as well as traded from Inuit in exchange for
goods brought to Greenland by Scandinavian ships.

Archaeological work on the tip of Baffin Island at the entrance
to Hudson Strait is another comparison to the very inconclusive
testing at Runestone Hill in Minnesota. Between 1576 and 1578,
Englishman Martin Frobisher led three expeditions searching for
the fabled Northwest Passage through America to China (it doesn't
exist, but it took centuries to determine this). On his first voyage in
1576, Frobisher collected rock samples erroneously identified as
gold ore. Iron ore was also discovered and correctly identified. The
next two voyages concentrated on mining the "gold," only to be dis-
graced when their cargoes of tons of ore were proved to be valueless.
Frobisher subsequently resumed his career as a privateer. Meanwhile, the crews occupied substantial camps on a bare island in Frobisher Bay. Inuit of the region took their discards, supplies they had
cached for the next season, and clothing and artifacts stripped from
dead Englishmen who were murdered when they intruded into
Inuit hunting grounds.

Stories of the large band of Englishmen were told for generations in Inuit communities. In 1861 an American explorer, Charles
Hall, traveled in the region searching for the remains of the lost Sir
John Franklin expedition of 1845–48. Hall respectfully befriended
local Inuit, learning their language and traveling with them.
Instead of bringing him to Franklin's wreck, they took him to Frobisher's site, astonishing Hall with their oral historical knowledge
of "kadlunat" (Europeans) nearly three centuries earlier. Inuit still
called the little island Kodlunarn, "White man's place." Hall collected artifacts and mapped ruins from the Frobisher activities,
depositing half in the Smithsonian Institution in Washington, D.C.,
and half in an English museum. When Hall published his account
soon after his return, readers were thrilled by his Inuit life experi-
ences but not much interested in the Frobisher voyage—a story of
foolish dreams of gold, iron mines, and an ocean strait that ended
not in fabulous China but in Hudson's Bay.

Fast forward a century to Smithsonian researchers interested in analyzing one of Hall's lumps of Elizabethan iron using a recently developed method of obtaining radiocarbon estimates from charcoal mixed with the smelted iron. Were the lumps of iron possibly Norse, or Frobisher's, or later? The answer, it would seem, is Norse: two samples dated to A.D. 1240–1400 and A.D. 1160–1280.

Here archaeology refuses to agree with radiocarbon tests. The site's location, Inuit oral history, ruins of a stone structure the Englishmen built to test whether it would outlast a winter, a trench dug to pull up a boat, and Elizabethan-type artifacts all conform well with details in the book published by one of Frobisher's officers. Nothing looked Norse, except nondescript iron blooms (lumps of smelted and hammered iron) and slag. Scientists working with the Frobisher project considered whether Frobisher's smiths may have made charcoal from Kodlunarn driftwood, which could have come from as far away as Siberia over the Arctic Ocean and been preserved by the cold. But on his second and third voyages, Frobisher carried tons of charcoal to be used in smelting, and that charcoal would have been made from sixteenth-century wood, especially branches and younger trees not suited for building timber. The analysts concurred that given Greenlandic Norse iron production and travel for hunting and lumber, Norse artifacts in the Canadian High Arctic, and the bog-iron smithy at L'Anse aux Meadows, the iron blooms might have been manufactured by Norse a couple of centuries before Frobisher. Kodlunarn is a prominent local landmark and defensible campsite. Could Norse have carried the iron blooms, weighing nearly 28, 24, and 12 pounds, in their boats as ballast, offloading them when preparing to return with the products of their hunts? One fact works against the blooms being medieval Norse: their chemical components match British, not Scandinavian, ore sources. Therefore, it appears that Frobisher carried lumps of iron already a couple of centuries old! The best explanation offered by archaeologist Robert Ehrenreich, a consultant to the Frobisher project, is that the heavy lumps were used in ship construction and repair, placed against the head of a nail or rivet to prevent it jerking back when its point was clinched. Nearly indestructible, the blooms may have been used by generations of shipwrights and put on board Frobisher's ship when it was outfitted, then left on Kodlunarn in expectation of returning the following year (Ehrenreich in Fitzhugh and Olin 1993:228).

L'Anse aux Meadows and Frobisher's camp on Kodlunarn Island are exceptionally well-preserved, undisturbed, and documented sites. Although it took Helge Ingstad many years of sailing, reconnoitering coasts, and reconciling diverse medieval documents to deduce L'Anse aux Meadows was probably Leif Eiriksson's Vinland, his exhaustive presentation of his evidence is compelling. Both sites were investigated over several seasons by teams of experienced archaeologists and consultants with technical expertise. They contrast with Kensington's Runestone Hill, lacking any features evident on or below the surface and yielding only a very small collection of nondescript artifacts. That little is assumed to have been chipped by American Indians, but it should be noted that medieval Scandinavians continued chipping stone for tool blades as did their prehistoric forebears (Knarrström 2001). No one has sourced the flakes from Runestone Hill. It could be that Goths and Norwegians there in 1362 used local stone to make new blades for tools. Archaeology works best with sites occupied for at least several months by at least several dozen people, making structures and distinctively styled artifacts that they readily lose or discard. None of these characteristics apply to the postulated ephemeral camp on Runestone Hill.

Chapter Four

The Hard Data
Geology

Was the Kensington Runestone carved in 1362 or the 1890s? If 1362, the runes should be weathered. Are they? This basic question was investigated in 1909–10 by Minnesota's foremost geologist, Newton Winchell. Winchell was born in 1839. His older brother became a professor of natural history—geology, zoology, and botany—at the University of Michigan, and Newton earned bachelor's and master's degrees from that institution, assisting his brother in his research. In 1872, he was appointed to direct the new Minnesota Geological and Natural History Survey, a position he held until 1900. He also taught geology and mineralogy at the University of Minnesota. He was a founding member of the Geological Society of America and of its journal, its president in 1902, and editor of *American Geologist* until 1905. He spent a year and a half in France broadening his research competence in petrology. Clearly, Winchell brought unparalleled experience to the Runestone investigation, heightened by a reputation for "great diligence and honesty" (Merrill 1964:376). An entry in a biographical dictionary sums him up as "an honest, very competent geologist" (Thrapp 1990:1581).

Apparently it was Hjalmar Holand who urged the Minnesota Historical Society to appoint a committee to evaluate the Runestone. The Society asked a minister who wrote on the Bible, who was also an avocational archaeologist, to chair the committee. It was rounded out by another theologian, an advertising man who had assisted Major John Wesley Powell's mapping of the Colorado River, Winchell, and Warren Upham, a Society staff member with extensive geological fieldwork. Winchell characteristically plunged into field investigation for four days at the end of November 1909 and followed with two three-day visits in March 1910. Recording observations, sketch maps, and interviews in a pocket field notebook, Winchell carefully walked the Ohman and neighboring farms, collecting and identifying specimen rocks, reading the lay of the land to image how it would have looked in 1362, checking nearby lakes for resemblance to the text "camp by 2 skerries one days journey north," and talking at length with local farmers, businesspeople, and clergy. On March 5, 1910, Winchell recorded, "I had a long talk with Mr. Ohman, and am impressed with the evident candor and truthfulness of all his statements, and also I find he is a more intellectual man than I had supposed" (quoted in Blegen 1968:153).

Winchell's knowledge of Minnesota graywacke informed his evaluation of the weathering of the runes. His estimation of age was supported by Upham and by William Hotchkiss, Wisconsin's state geologist, whom he brought into the examination. Although the magnification available in 1909 was low compared to Scott Wolter's technology in 2000, the white lines of nail scratching to clean out the incising in 1898 stand in bright contrast to the dark, rough-edged runes, evidencing years of weathering after carving. This direct testimony of the rock, plus Winchell's thorough interviewing in the Kensington region and his recognition that Runestone Hill likely was an island centuries ago (it rests above a marsh), led him to conclude that there was strong support for an authentic Runestone date of 1362 and little reason to suspect fraud.

The Minnesota Historical Society committee initially resolved to report, "that this Committee regards the genuineness of the supposed Kensington Rune Stone as not established, but that they deem the preponderance of evidence to be in favor of the Stone" (quoted in Blegen 1968:89). Then in July, after much discussion, the committee decided against forwarding this opinion to the Society's executive council, instead submitting for publication the statement, "the Council and Society reserve their conclusion until more agreement of opinions for or against it" (quoted in Blegen 1968:91). Nearly uniform disparagement of text and runes by professional linguists overruled the geologists.

Olof Ohman (right), Nils Flaten (middle), and neighbor on top of knoll where Runestone was discovered. Photo taken about 1910.

Surely it is significant that a *historical* society rejected Winchell's, Hotchkiss', and Upham's evaluation based on geological data and experience. On its appointed committee, language-oriented members—two theologians and an advertising man—outnumbered the pair of geologists. Its executive council had a similar predominance of people who worked with texts, not the observational data of the sciences. This likely inclined the council to weigh linguists' opinions, using canons of criticism with which they were familiar, over presentations by scientists. What the council and those who followed its conclusion failed to realize was the fundamental difference at that time between text evaluation and physical science: linguists constructed a standard language based on formal documents, excluding non-conforming texts, while geologists and other natural scientists collected ranges of data. A generation later, professor Leonard Bloomfield propounded a more scientific method for linguistics based on collecting ranges of real speech. For a scientific linguist such as Robert Hall, the Kensington inscription was a particular, therefore unique, text in the same way the rock itself, a slab of glacially transported Animikie graywacke, is unique in its particulars. Scientific analysis matches the *preponderance* of data to a general model or widely known type example, leaving some attributes in a residual category likely unique to the specimen or local collection.

The scientists who examined the Runestone a century after its discovery were puzzled by the Minnesota Historical Society's decision to prefer linguists' opinion to the geologists' conclusion. Richard Nielsen, Barry Hanson, and Scott Wolter all independently visited the Historical Society archives to examine Winchell's fieldnotes. They each saw that his work had been exemplary. For the Historical Society executive council to put a disclaimer on his conclusion and disregard it resembled medieval scholars refusing to accept the conclusions of Copernicus, Kepler, and Galileo that the earth revolves around the sun. To the "hard" scientists, the possibility was extremely low that the meticulous Winchell, with decades of experience collecting and analyzing Minnesota rock as well as a sterling reputation in his field, was in error in concluding that the runes showed weathering inconsistent with a settler-era carving. Their own eyeballing of the stone, of course, suggested the same.

Nielsen and Hanson sought expertise for a contemporary examination of the Runestone using today's high-tech instruments. They selected American Petrographic Services in St. Paul, Minnesota, run by geologist Scott Wolter. Wolter had never heard of the Kensington Runestone, but once it was explained, the project seemed straightforward. He began his work in July 2000. Like Winchell, Wolter went out to the discovery site to observe the area's topography, basic geology, and glacial effects. LuAnn Patton, director of the Runestone Museum, agreed to allow the stone to be transported to St. Paul, and Wolter examined it in his laboratory in October 2000. He presented the results of that work in early November to the Midwest/Plains Archaeological Conference meeting that year in St. Paul. Subsequently, Wolter presented slides of his data and his interpretations to his peers at a meeting of Twin Cities professional geologists; lively discussion ensued on the rate of disintegration of mica crystals in the graywacke, but the basic point that the rune carvings showed weathering was not disputed.

Wolter's March 2004 summary report begins with a detailed description of the stone slab. Fiber-optic light directed at a low angle across the rough, uncarved back side of the stone revealed striations indicating a glacier had pushed across the graywacke bedrock and pulled the slab out, carrying it within the ice southwestward across Minnesota until, about 12,000 to 15,000 years ago, the ice melted, depositing the slab in the hillocky, marshy region of Kensington. On the same back side of the rock are two white lines crossing the striations; these were caused by roots growing around the slab. The lines are not as wide as the aspen roots seen by the Ohmans and Flaten because they were made by root tip fungi excreting acid that reacted with minerals in the rock, releasing nutrients to the plant—as the roots matured, the leaching action on the rock stopped as the tips grew beyond the slab and bark formed around the roots' older portions. The pair of root-leached lines matches the drawings of the roots around the slab made by the Ohmans and their neighbors.

Regarding the Runestone's overall weathering, Wolter states,

> An important aspect of the stone is the weathering character of the different surfaces. All of the surfaces that have been weathering since being transported and then deposited by glaciers have a similar appearance. . . . The split side surface has a darker overall gray color and does not exhibit the prominent pitting observed on the glacial surfaces. This surface appears to have been exposed to weathering for a significantly shorter length of time [than the 12,000 years since the glacier melted]. (Wolter 2004:17)

Looking at the runes, Wolter saw when the stone was recovered, the nail used to clean it had removed "weathering products" and crushed the minerals under the forceful pressure, creating the white appearance:

> The color and texture of the areas adjacent to the deepest part of the retooled grooves . . . have the same darker gray color as the split side of the stone, and represent areas where flakes of rock spalled off immediately adjacent to the main grooves at the time the stone was originally carved. (Wolter 2004:19)
>
> Roughly a dozen characters on the split side of the stone do not appear to have been retooled . . . these original characters have the same color, texture and weathering features as the entire side into which they were carved. . . . These characters are important because they exhibit weathering features such as iron oxide deposits . . . developed from the decomposition of the mineral pyrite (FeS_2). . . . Within some of the original grooves are small (~0.5 mm) iron oxide-coated pits that represent pyrite crystals that have completely weathered away. (Wolter 2004:23)

A genuine hoax confessed to in 2001 proved useful to Wolter. In 1985, five graduate students taking a course in rune texts at the University of Minnesota went to see the Kensington Runestone in the museum at Alexandria. The young people decided to carve AVM (as on the Kensington Stone) and runes for 1363 on a rock near Runestone Hill to see whether it would be discovered and what discoverers would think of it. The stone was noticed late in 1994 by a group of area farmers interested in the Kensington Runestone. By the next spring it was determined to be a hoax. Six years later, in the spring of 2001, Robert Johnson, a retired geologist, and his daughter Janey Westin, a professional stonecarver, were walking over the knoll looking for evidence of a Norse camp when Westin spotted the AVM rock in a pile of stones cleared off a field by the farmer. Excitement ensued, the find was discussed in the Twin Cities, and archaeological testing for summer 2001 was contracted and carried out, until two of the students, both now professors in other states, wrote to the Minnesota Historical Society, admitting the hoax. Scott Wolter had by this time seen that in contrast to the Kensington Stone, the "AVM Stone" displayed actively oxidizing pyrite crystals in its carvings. He was delighted by the confession of the 1985 hoax, because now the AVM Stone provided data on the rate of weathering of pyrite crystals in the Kensington environment. Pyrite in the Kensington rune carvings had oxidized completely, leaving little pits visible under Wolter's microscope. Since the pyrites on the AVM Stone carving were not weathered away after nearly twenty years in the open on the stone pile, the Kensington runes must have been exposed considerably longer—longer than Ohman had been living on his farm.

To more precisely identify the minerals in the rock and weathered surfaces, Wolter drilled out a narrow core from the back side of the Runestone. A colleague, Richard Ojakangas, examined thin sections of the core, comparing its minerals to those in other specimens of metagraywacke and found it matched a source in the Animikie basin of east-central Minnesota. That is, the rock is highly likely to have been transported by a glacier from eastern Minnesota, not carried by people from a distant origin.

Further testing required Wolter to take core and chip samples to the Materials Laboratory at Iowa State University, where equipment for scanning electron microscopy and energy-dispersive x-ray microanalysis had the advantage of not requiring, as other instruments do, that the samples be coated with other minerals. Results from these scans agreed with previous microscopy showing weathering. Paul Weiblen, a retired professor of geology at the University of Minnesota, also examined thin sections from the coring under his department's electron microscope. He agreed with Wolter and

Winchell that although most of the minerals in the graywacke are resistant to weathering, some mineral grains do, and did, react with atmosphere and soil, becoming rounded or disintegrating. All three geologists concur that the condition of the runes indicates many years of weathering.

Studies of weathering on tombstones could assist researchers in estimating how long the runes had been weathering. Wolter searched for such studies but, to his surprise, found very little. He subsequently began his own data library. In March 2003, he went to southern Maine—climate there is similar to that in Kensington but since colonization started there in the eighteenth century, he might find tombstones much older than any in Minnesota. With permission from caretakers, he collected chip samples from tombstones dated from 1796 to 1865. Three tombstones, dated 1805, 1806, and 1815, contained mica grains like those in the Kensington Runestone. Scanned under the electron microscope, the tombstone mica exhibited deterioration but not as advanced as on the Kensington stone. Therefore, this comparison indicated the Kensington split surface and carved runes are older than 200 years.

This one comparative study is not sufficient to establish relative dating for the Runestone, as Wolter recognizes. He has begun assiduously collecting tombstones and chip samples from tombstones, and soliciting such data from other geologists. On a trip to Wisconsin, Wolter phoned me and I suggested we drive to Lizard Mounds Park, a fascinating effigy mounds site near Milwaukee. Out on the county highway, Wolter spied a small pioneer cemetery and pulled over. Several tombstones dated in the mid-nineteenth century lay discarded in a corner. We knocked on the door of a nearby house and were told that the cemetery caretaker did not know where the fallen tombstones belonged and would not allow them to be set up, so the house resident felt confident no one would object to the geologist taking them for his research. Wolter left a couple of his business cards, assuring the resident that he would immediately return the stones should there be objection, and after photographing and taking notes on the standing tombstones and physical environment, loaded the discards in his pickup. I should mention that this was a January day, sunny but windy and bitterly cold; although we were both wearing heavy parkas, it took love of research to keep us out there for an hour at near-zero temperature.

In June 2004, Wolter brought the Kensington Runestone to Stockholm, Sweden, for examination there by geologist Runo Löfvendahl and a group of scientists he brought in. Their task, they stated, was to test Wolter's interpretation of observations by bringing up alternative explanations, for example that the white lines on the back of the Runestone resulted from water channeled through the subsoil rather than leaching from roots. (Wolter's reply to this was that several witnesses to the find in 1898 independently sketched a pair of roots clasped around the back of the stone, just where the pair of white lines cross.) The Swedish team disappointed Wolter by not subjecting the runestone to scanning electron microscopy to determine whether they would get results similar to those he obtained in America by this technology. They seemed reluctant to pursue the question; although they claimed they were using the scientific methodological principle of "falsificationism" (playing devil's advocate), they stopped short of the concluding methodological step of "inference to the best explanation"; of stating, as Wolter had, the interpretation that seems to best fit the data.

Scott Wolter's business is forensic petrography; "autopsies of stone," as he puts it. Most of his company's work involves claims, frequently legal, about faulty construction or damage. On September 22, 2001, American Petrographic Services—that is, Scott Wolter—was invited to join in analysis of the damage sustained by the Pentagon after the terrorists' hijacked plane crashed into it on September 11. Wolter's customers respected his commitment to put their assignments aside until the Pentagon project was completed, a job that took his laboratory until nearly the end of December. The tests resulted in a recommendation that the damaged section of the Pentagon be torn out and rebuilt rather than making many spot repairs, a decision that expedited reconstruction and saved taxpayer money. The Pentagon work speaks to Scott Wolter's reputation among engineers requiring petrographic analyses and implies that his evaluation of the Kensington Runestone carving's age is scientifically sound.

Chapter Five

Linguistics
Recognizing Medieval
Dialect Variation

Beginning with Olaus Breda early in 1899, the authenticity of the Kensington Runestone inscription has been denied because its language and runes allegedly differ from what would have been used by Norsemen in 1362. Hjalmar Holand took the opposite position, that the inscription tells us more than had been known in 1899 about the variety of language dialects and runes used in 1362. Most of the Scandinavian professors of Norse linguistics—that is, men who enjoyed the status of authorities on medieval Norse languages and writing—defended their expertise by dismissing the Runestone's anomalies as evidence of an inexpert forger.

Anomalies are at once the bane and the fun of science. Thomas Kuhn, a historian of science, wrote in his pithy *The Structure of Scientific Revolutions* (1962) that each scientific field holds models of what defines good science in that discipline, in terms of both method and explanation. Students are trained to follow their professors' procedures and to explain phenomena using principles and premises accepted as valid by those professors. Kuhn said that most scientists are puzzle-solvers whose puzzles are presented to them by leading researchers, rather like crossword puzzles where you figure out how to fill in the little blanks without wondering whether the puzzle itself may be flawed. Over time, Kuhn claimed, anomalies—observations that are unexpected and seem to conflict with accepted models— accumulate in a scientific field, until someone realizes that the standard model (Kuhn called them "paradigms") is wrong and has the nerve to challenge the authorities. Kuhn used examples from astronomy, namely the medieval model that the solar system revolves around the earth and the challenges posed by Copernicus, Kepler, and Galileo that argued for a heliocentric model with the earth and other planets revolving around the sun. It was revolutionary when a long-standing model was successfully rejected in favor of a radically different one. While Kuhn did not go into the personal crises such a revolution would create, sociologist-of-science Barry Barnes looked into those personal dimensions, pointing out how leaders might fear that their status and perks would be diminished if they followed a rival (Barnes 1977; see also Barnes, Bloor, and Henry 1996).

From that perspective, it isn't surprising that recent research on the Runestone was initiated by two scientists whose income and status lie in quite different fields. Neither Richard Nielsen nor Barry Hanson would lose anything other than self-esteem if their ventures proved foolish. By the same token, Minnesota and Smithsonian historians and archaeologists who have been loath to reject the hoax identity of the Runestone are loath to risk their reputations. Barry Barnes reminds us that what is often at stake is money for research support and job raises and even job security. There is a lesson in the slurs suffered for many years by Hjalmar Holand.

J. A. Holvik pursued debunking the Runestone as tirelessly as Holand sought to persuade acceptance. Holvik, like Holand, was proudly Norwegian-American. Holvik taught Norwegian language and also band and golf at Concordia College in Moorhead, Minnesota. He worked fervently to promote Norwegians' contributions to America, his efforts recognized in 1925 (the announced centennial of Norwegian settlements in America) by the government of Norway dubbing him a knight in the Order of St. Olaf. Students and staff at Concordia remembered Holvik launching an impassioned tirade against the Runestone's authenticity on any and every occasion.

Holvik was only a student when, in 1910, he assisted the Winchell committee by comparing the Runestone runes with those given in the Swedish grammar owned by itinerant minister and teacher Sven Fogelblad. Holvik reported to Winchell that the number of deviations and errors in the Runestone inscription show that whoever chiseled the inscription was not relying on the textbook. Forty years later, late in 1949, Holvik went to the Ohman farm asking to see Olof's books. Olof's daughter Amanda complied, and Holvik discovered, and published, that in addition to the Almquist grammar originally owned by Fogelblad, Ohman had another Swedish textbook, *Der Kunskapsrike Skolmastaren* by Rosander. This book, Holvik thought, did provide enough material to compose the Kensington inscription. The other missile in Holvik's armament against the Runestone was his claim that the poor copy of the inscription sent to the Minneapolis newspaper *Svenska Amerikanska Posten* was not a copy but a preliminary *draft* that had been imperfectly corrected before it was used as text for the (hoax) inscription.

It's curious that the proud Norwegian Holvik campaigned so hard against evidence that Norwegians had been the first Europeans to explore deep inside America. Of course Olof Ohman and the eight Goths in the inscription were Swedes, but the inscription says the majority in the 1362 party were Norwegians. Hjalmar Holand was, like Holvik, Norwegian-American. Research on Holvik by a Concordia College professor turned up letters telling of a quarrel between Holvik and Holand at a meeting in Norway in 1911. Holvik said that belief in the Runestone's authenticity discredited Norwegian-Americans, making them appear fools and that he was upholding the intelligence of his ethnic group when denouncing (the Swedes) Ohman, Fogelblad, and Hedberg. For Holvik, Holand's tenacity in seeking data to support the Runestone was maddeningly embarrassing.

When Erik Wahlgren, a professor of Scandinavian languages and literature at the University of California–Los Angeles, wrote to Holvik about his 1949 discovery, he was eager to cooperate. Wahlgren's academic respectability gave weight to Holvik's arguments. Much of Wahlgren's 1958 very negative book on the Runestone builds upon Holvik's work, giving considerably more space to his version of the history of the find than to linguistics. Wahlgren denigrates not only Holand but also Newton Winchell, reading the geologist's consultations with Holand on discovery evidence and interpretation of runes to indicate improper influence, somehow, by the young historian upon the eminent geologist. Holvik died in 1960, Holand in 1963 (not long after he rebutted Wahlgren).

Linguistics came back into the picture in 1982 with the publication of a concise book by a professor of philology from Cornell, Robert A. Hall, Jr. Hall was not of Scandinavian descent nor a

Minnesotan, simply a highly trained and experienced linguistics researcher bothered by deficiencies in reasoning. Hall set forth basic scientific method, emphasizing (like your present author) where the weight of probability falls. Although Romance rather than Scandinavian linguistics was his specialty, he was sufficiently familiar with that related Indo-European language group to evaluate claims pro and con in light of recent scholarship. Hall had been a student of Leonard Bloomfield, a major figure in twentieth-century linguistics known for his uncompromising insistence on highly detailed phonetic recording of languages and on analyses proceeding according to explicit principles and methodology. Bloomfield had studied at the University of Wisconsin only a few years after Holand, concentrating on linguistics and working on American Indian and Philippine languages as well as German. Hall, like his teacher, spent much of his professional life researching language histories and analyzing sound and syntax changes through time. Dismissing the Runestone inscription because it didn't conform to academics' concept of standard Old Norse ran counter to Bloomfield's fruitful work on dialects in both spoken and written forms.

Setting out the problem, Hall separated linguistic and graphemic (written, i.e., the runes) issues from those concerning geology, dendrology (questions about the tree clasping the stone), and historical circumstances of both 1898 and 1362. Here, we will look at Hall's discussion of the linguistic issues, his area of expertise. Because he himself was not a specialist on medieval Norse, Hall used a 1950 study of the inscription by Sivert Hagen, a work he evaluates as "a very solid piece of philological investigation . . . but badly neglected" by Blegen, and attacked by Wahlgren on grounds other than linguistics (Hall 1982:13). Hall, whose principal scholarly topics included borrowings between languages and the emergence of creoles (languages developed in bilingual communities), was particularly interested in Hagen's comments on alleged American English forms in the Kensington inscription. Hagen came from a Scandinavian immigrant community contemporary with Ohman's and wrote, "I never heard any Americanized Swede or Norwegian use a mixture like the one which seems so plausible from the point of view of scholars in the Scandinavian countries" (quoted in Hall 1982:14).

Under the heading "Anachronisms," Hall launched into a technical discussion of the rune read as "h," which Hall suggests could

be a *Grenzsignal* or "open juncture" sound occurring in "pre-pausal
or other positions, and can include partial or complete de-voicing"
(Hall 1982:16). Thirty-four more pages of such technical considerations follow, detailing attestations of medieval variations in runes
and finding all but one of the Kensington runes in scholarly com-
pendia published by mid-twentieth century. In a revised edition
published in 1994, Hall cited hundreds of rune inscriptions on
pieces of wood recovered from medieval Bergen, Norway; these, not
available to scholars until the 1980s, demonstrated how very common it had been for ordinary people to carve short texts and how
varied their runes were. Hall, like Hagen, was impressed by the
Kensington inscription's presentation of a relatively long text con-
sistently using phonemes (recognized speech sounds) of a distinct
dialect. In common with most rune writers of the fourteenth century, this carver struggled to identify or modify runes to fit actual
speech, thus giving to posterity a great range of variation and idio-
syncratic usages. Fourteenth-century literate Scandinavians were
familiar, too, with Latin (the language of the church) and Latin
inscriptions with words neatly carved in regular rows. The man
who carved the Kensington inscription had no library of manuscripts or scribes to consult; he did his best to create a clear vernacular text that his countrymen would be able to read, should they
come later.

Just as Thomas Kuhn and Barry Barnes would have pre-
dicted, Robert Hall's credentials as a leading Bloomfieldian linguist
served him well within the scientific community of linguistics, but
carried no comparable weight with non-linguists. Hall's technical
language (for example, "the //gh// of //pagh// stands for the fricative
allophone [y] of /g/" [Hall 1982:17]) lies outside historians' and
archaeologists' modes of discourse. This is glaring in the expen-
sively produced book *Vikings: The North Atlantic Saga* (2000), with
a preface by Hillary Rodham Clinton, published to accompany a
blockbuster traveling museum exhibit by that name. Although
1362 is centuries past the Viking period, the book includes two sections on the Kensington Runestone, stating it "is universally considered a hoax by scholars today . . . scholars can easily debunk" it
(Ward in Fitzhugh and Ward 2000:367) and that the Smithsonian
Institution has a form letter "written in unambiguous terms saying
that scholarly opinion has judged the Kensington Stone to be a
nineteenth-century creation" (Wallace and Fitzhugh in Fitzhugh

and Ward 2000:383). Hall's book is listed in the bibliography, compiled by an assistant, but neither he nor "linguistics" is in the index. Birgitta Wallace and William Fitzhugh, mature scholars themselves, tell the public, "Despite nearly universal scholarly disdain, the Kensington Stone continues to be promoted by a few defenders [naming Hall along with Landsverk, Nielsen, and Nilsestuen] whose most successful argument against these Scandinavian conclusions is that specialists on runes and Nordic languages are prejudiced against laymen" (Wallace and Fitzhugh in Fitzhugh and Ward 2000:382). To characterize Robert A. Hall, Jr. as a "layman" and completely ignore his analysis within the paradigm of scientific linguistics is, in a word, irresponsible.

Richard Nielsen is an amateur in medieval Scandinavian linguistics, but over two decades of focused research and extensive correspondence with academic specialists including Robert Hall, he gained familiarity with the technical literature. Nielsen, who grew up in a Danish-speaking home in California, earned master's degrees in applied mathematics and in engineering from the University of Michigan and a doctorate in materials science from the University of Denmark, Copenhagen. His interest in the Kensington Runestone controversy developed during the years he lived in Scandinavia working as a consulting engineer. Returning to the United States in 1985, he began systematically amassing and collating variations in runes and words in medieval Scandinavian manuscripts and inscriptions. He prepared tables listing the "errors" and "English words" highlighted by naysayers beginning with Olaus Breda, as well as instances of these forms in more recently published collections and dictionaries. In this manner, Nielsen asserts that these runes and words were in use at least somewhere in medieval northern Europe and could have been known to a fourteenth-century Swede or Norwegian. Particularly, Nielsen cites dialect studies placing several Runestone words in fourteenth-century Bohuslän speech, in western Sweden.

Nielsen's critics take issue with some of the correspondences he sees between Kensington runes and Scandinavian medieval runes, claiming that there are discernible differences. For those words, critics offer alternate medieval forms or sequences of shifts in sound or grammar. Underlying much of the contention is a deep-seated difference of opinion discussed by another of Leonard Bloomfield's outstanding students in scientific linguistics, Charles Hockett:

> *Analytic Norms.* . . . a question for which there is currently no
> clear answer: the choice between *frequency norms* and *clarity
> norms* in phonologic [sound] analysis. . . . In most languages, if
> not in all, there is a prescribed pattern for extra-clear speech, to
> which one resorts when normal rapid speech is not understood,
> or when certain social factors [for example, legal situations]
> prescribe it. . . . Frequency-norm analysis insists, in theory, on
> accepting for analysis any utterance which is produced by a na-
> tive speaker and understood, or understandable, by other na-
> tive speakers. . . . Most of the time, then, in the actual workings
> of language, what is actually said differs, from what might have
> been said [extra-clearly] but wasn't, not just in one phonologic
> feature, but in many. (Hockett 1955:214, 220)

"Bloomfieldian" linguists are acutely attuned to actual speech, what
Hockett terms frequency norms, as opposed to eliciting conscious
standard forms (clarity norms). For Robert Hall and Sivert Hagen,
the Kensington Runestone inscription is a delight, a gift of a speech
by a fourteenth-century Götlander educated enough to strive to
write clearly but with no pretensions to formal court language. It is
what they expect from real speech. Nielsen, as an amateur linguist,
isn't involved in this methodological debate between schools of professionals, but fits with the Bloomfieldians.

These scientists are more comfortable with anomalies than are
those who seek clarity norms, the unambiguous, carefully structured
utterances. Clarity-norm devotees are puzzle-solvers in Thomas
Kuhn's metaphor of normal science. Frequency-norm advocates tend
toward what philosopher Charles Peirce in 1878 called "surprising
facts." Peirce asserted that every argument holds a Case, a Rule, and
a Result, permitting three basic procedures according to whether one
begins with the Rule (e.g., "Norse inscribed runestones") followed by
the Case ("The Kensington Stone is inscribed in Norse runes"); or
with the Case followed by the Result ("The Kensington Stone is
Norse"), then the Rule; or with the Rule followed by the Result and
then the Case. If you can walk through philosophers' logic, the point
Peirce and his admirers emphasize is that the third type of argument
begins with a hypothesis formulated as a *provisional* rule. We have
seen that simple deduction ("Norse inscribed runestones therefore
this runestone is Norse") wasn't acceptable because the simple argument failed to answer many related questions: Could Norse have
traveled to Minnesota in 1362? For what reason would Norse travel
to Minnesota in 1362? Is this Runestone recently carved? Simple

induction similarly fails, because the Case (the Kensington Stone) and the Result (Kensington is Norse) are supported by the Rule ("Norse carved runestones") only if it is reasonably established that the Case was carved in 1362. The advantage of framing the argument beginning with Rule as *hypothesis*, what Peirce termed "abduction," is that one is not doing a set crossword puzzle but rather is actively casting about for corollary propositions to determine whether the Case really belongs with the Rule and Result.

When Richard Nielsen sets out example after example of medieval runes and words that seem to duplicate or to suggest regularities that would encompass the Kensington text, he is providing Cases to support the Rule and Result that the Kensington Runestone is medieval. When opponents beginning with Breda in 1899 state that this, that, and the other word or rune in the Kensington inscription is not medieval Norse (or Old Swedish, or fourteenth-century Bohuslänsk), they are deducing that, given the Rule "this is medieval Norse," the Case does not fit the Rule and therefore the Case is *not* medieval Norse. When archaeologists such as the Smithsonian's William Fitzhugh use induction to begin with the Case "the Kensington Stone is Minnesota graywacke and lay in Minnesota," and the Rule "pre-Columbian inhabitants of Minnesota were American Indians," the only result they can accept, logically, is that the Kensington Runestone was not made in 1362. That is, American archaeologists and historians are talking about *a stone in Minnesota*, not about runic text. These archaeologists do not allow the Ingstads' validation of Norse settlement west of Greenland to sway the probability of Norse in Minnesota, choosing instead to emphasize that archaeology shows Norse hunting and trading only in the Canadian Maritimes and High Arctic.

Conversely, Breda et al. have been stating Rules about Norse texts and runes. The Minnesota Historical Society decided in 1910 to defer to that argument rather than to stick to geologist Winchell's argument of Rule—"weathered incisions on northern Minnesota graywacke indicate age in centuries"—to Result "Kensington Runestone incisions show weathering" to Case "the Kensington Runestone is centuries old." Robert A. Hall, Jr.'s argument *hypothesizes* a Rule "medieval runic inscriptions attest wide variation in rune characters and words," the opposite of the Rule stated by Breda et al. Hall has reason to begin with his hypothesized Rule, because it derives from his long experience analyzing frequency norms in European texts. He thought about alternative tests and considered geology and dendrology, finding both supported his hypothesis, adding weight to the probability that the Kensington Runestone is 1362 Norse.

Drawing out the logics of opposing schools is tedious to read, but it does illuminate how the groups talk past one another. It illustrates, too, how easy it is for opponents to repeat what they *know* (what is medieval Norse or only American Indians were in Minnesota before the nineteenth century) instead of seeking out additional tests for a hypothesis. Winchell also began with what he knew well, the rocks of northern Minnesota; he confirmed by surveying and collecting field rocks around Kensington that the Runestone graywacke probably had been carried there by a Pleistocene glacier, and so he and his geologist colleagues could test the hypothesis that the Runestone was carved in 1362 by examining weathering in the incised runes. Nearly a century later, Richard Nielsen and Barry Hanson, both with engineering experience grounded in hard science, understood the power of Winchell's interpretation and arranged for the stronger test of his hypothesis available with 1990s technology. Meanwhile, Nielsen continued working in the paradigm formulated by Robert Hall and his fellow Bloomfieldian linguists.

A brief note here to readers: linguists Umberto Eco (who is also a novelist) and Thomas Sebeok collected essays from colleagues and philosophers in a book, *The Sign of Three*, that reveals the surprising fact that Charles Peirce, an actual philosopher, and Sherlock Holmes, his fictional contemporary, used comparable logic in solving cases. Their essays are surely the most enjoyable way to learn about deductive, inductive, and abductive logic.

Linguistics allows wiggle-room because medieval manuscripts and carvings were not standardized like computer fonts. Is this tiny line a hook on a rune, or a slip of the quill pen or stonecarver's chisel? How was the word for "death"—or is it an adjective, "dead"—pronounced in Bohuslän in 1362, and by Götlanders traveling on trade expeditions? The Minnesota Historical Society figured, in 1910, that it would be a straightforward matter to rely on opinions by Scandinavian linguists. The majority of those asked thought little of the inscription. A much-expanded dictionary of Old Swedish and corpora of medieval texts have, since then, provided what look to Nielsen like matches to the Kensington text, but "not quite all" to his critics in Scandinavia. Historical linguistics, like archaeology, can validate a hypothesis with a positive instance, but cannot absolutely invalidate a hypothesis by a null finding: one does not know what is not discovered.

The Face:

1. ᛔ : ᚵᚯᛏᛂᚱ : ᚮᚴ : ᛚᛚ : ᚿᚮᚱᚱᛘᛂᚿ : ᛒᚮ :
8 : göter : ok : 22 : norrmen : po :
Åtta göter and tjugotvå norrmän på
Eight Götalanders and 22 Norwegians on

2. ᚮᛒᚦᛆᚵᛂᛚᛋᛂᚠᛆᚱᚦ : ᚠᚱᚮ :
opþagelsefarþ : fro :
upptagelsefärd (= uppodlings- eller plundringsresa) från
reclaiming (or plundering) journey from

3. ᛘᛁᚿᛚᛆᚿᚦ : ᚮᚠ : ᛘᛂᛋᛏ : ᛘᛁ :
vinlanþ : of : vest : vi :
Vinland västerut. Vi
from Vinland to the west. We

4. ᚼᛆᚦᛂ : ᛚᛅᚵᛂᚱ : ᛘᛂᚦ : ᛚ : ᛋᚴᚠᛆᚱ : ᛂᚿ :
haþe : läger : veþ : 2 : skȽar : en :
hade läger vid två (???) en
had a camp by two (???) one

5. ᚦᛆᚵᛋ : ᚱᛁᛋᛂ : ᚿᚮᚱᚱ : ᚠᚱᚮ : ᚦᛂᚿᚮ : ᛋᛏᛂᚿ :
þags : rise : norr : fro : þeno : sten :
dagsresa norrut från denna sten.
day's journey north from this stone.

6. ᛘᛁ : ᛘᛆᚱ : ᚮᚴ : ᚠᛁᛋᚴᛂ : ᛂᚿ : ᚦᛆᚵᚼ : ᛅᛒᛏᛁᚱ :
vi : var : ok : fiske : en : þagh : äptir :
Vi var och (= för att) fiska en dag. Efter (att)
We were fishing one day. After

7. ᛘᛁ : ᚴᚮᛘ : ᚼᛂᛘ : ᚠᛆᚿ : ᛕ : ᛘᛆᚿ : ᚱᚯᚦᛂ :
vi : kom : hem : fan : 10 : man : röþe :
vi kom hem fann vi tio man röda
we came home we found 10 men red

8. ᛆᚠ : ᛒᛚᚮᚦ : ᚮᚵ : ᚦᛂᚦ : AVM :
af : bloþ : og : þeþ : AVM :
av blod och död. Ave Maria.
from blood and death. Ave Maria

9. ᚠᚱᛅᛂᛚᛋᛂ : ᛆᚠ : ᛁᛚᛚᚤ :
fräelse : af : illü :
Frälse av ondo.
Save from evil.

The Side:

10.ᛅᚼᛦ : ᛈ : ᛦᚷᛠᚼ : ᛦᛏ : ᛅᚷᛦᛏᛏ : ᚷᛏ : ᚼᛏ :
här : 10 : mans : ve : havet : at : se :
(Det) är tio man vid havet för att se
There are 10 men by the sea to look

11.ᚼᛒᛏᛁᛦ : ᛦᛱᛦᛏ : ᚼᛱᛁᛒ : ᚠᚵ : ᛆᚷᛦᛣ : ᛦᛁᚼᛏ :
äptir : vore : skip : 14 : þagh : rise :
efter våra skepp fjorton dag(ars) resa
after our ships fourteen days journey

12.ᚠᛦᛱᛦ : ᛆᛏᛱᛑ : ᚌᛣ : ᚷᛣᛦ : ᚠᚵᚠᚵ :
from : þeno : öh : ahr : 1362 :
från denna ö. År 1362.
from this island. Year 1362.

Some words or expressions were unknown to be Old Swedish or Swedish in 1898, but subsequently have been discovered to be Old Swedish:

rise (journey), line 5. First recorded in the Söderwall's Old Swedish Dictionary only in 1954.

from and **fraam** (from), line 12. Swedish dialect from Estonian colonies on the islands of Orm and Nukk documented in 1882 but only identified in relation to the Runestone by Richard Nielsen in January 2004.

þeno (this), lines 5 and 12. First recorded in Prof. Adolf Noreen's Old Swedish Grammar only in 1904.

AVM : fräelse : af : illü : (Ave Maria save from evil), lines 8–9. The hybrid prayer (Ave Maria save from evil) was only discovered as existing in Sweden during the 1300s and 1400s in the Matins of the St. Brigitta nunneries. This fact was only discovered in November 2003 by Henrik Williams. AV is a runic abbreviation for Ave.

The KRS Inscription by Prof. Henrik Williams, professor of Scandinavian languages, Uppsala University, Sweden, and Dr. Richard Nielsen of Houston, Texas.

Chapter Six

Biology
Tuberculosis? Blond Mandans? Red-haired Giants?

American anthropologists consider their discipline to have four components: cultural anthropology, archaeology, linguistic anthropology, and biological anthropology. Early in the twentieth century, influential professor Franz Boas insisted on keeping the four fields represented in anthropology departments and requiring graduate students to take at least introductory courses in each. Ideally, anthropologists themselves would actively research in each field during their careers, but even Boas and his exemplary student Alfred L. Kroeber came up a bit short of this goal. Although no anthropologist today approaches Boas and Kroeber in breadth of primary research, we uphold the principle of an integrative approach to human studies.

The "mystery" of the Kensington Runestone has aspects approached using biological anthropology. One longstanding question concerns the Mandan Nation on the Missouri River in central North Dakota. Another more recent angle brings in a remarkable mural painted in a Wisconsin rock shelter. The Ho-Chunk (formerly called the Winnebago), the Indian nation holding much of southwestern Wisconsin in the eighteenth century, recognize that the

51

rock shelter paintings illustrate part of their legendary history, according to which their hero Red Horn battled red-haired giants and married a woman of this race. It might seem that this story could refer to Ho-Chunk meeting Norse; if so, it would indicate a Norse presence at the time of L'Anse aux Meadows, much earlier than 1362, for the mural is radiocarbon-dated about A.D. 1000. A possibly related biological event is an epidemic of tuberculosis in the Upper Midwest at this time.

TUBERCULOSIS IN THE AMERICAN MIDWEST AROUND A.D. 1000

Tuberculosis is an infection by a bacterium, *Mycobacterium tuberculosis*. Most people exposed to this organism develop immunity, some become quite sick and die, and about five percent are sick for years, the infection causing lesions on their bones. This percentage can be detected by biological anthropologists analyzing skeletons excavated by archaeologists. The research is complicated by the possibility that common mycobacteria other than *M. tuberculosis* might have infected the bodies and caused skeletal lesions, or that the infection was a fungus, *Blastomyces dermatitidis*, which can similarly affect bones. Poor nutrition weakens people, making them less capable of resisting infection, and crowded living conditions with garbage accumulation increases exposure to infections. A population excavated from cemeteries by an archaeologist may appear healthy because it was well nourished and kept its homes and village clean. If living conditions deteriorate (as under warfare), resistance is lowered and infections persist, leaving marks on bones.

Around A.D. 1000, populations in the Midwest suffered an epidemic that left lesions on many skeletons. These look like tubercular infections; some, especially in warmer climates such as those from a site in Tennessee, could be *Blastomyces*. What look like tubercular lesions have been recognized on skeletons from southern coastal Peru and its north-central highlands, from prehistoric Pueblos in the American Southwest, as well as from a number of sites in the Midwest. The coastal Peru case was a naturally mummified body from which DNA could be extracted; samples from lung and lymph were identified to be *Mycobacterium tuberculosis*. The same bacterium was identified from DNA from a lesion on Wyoming bison bone dated to 15,000 B.C. This finding suggests tuberculosis may have been shared by bovines—cattle in Eurasia and bison in America—at the time the Americas were first being colonized by humans. The 16,000-year gap between the Pleistocene and wide-spread human occurrences in America makes it unlikely that *Mycobacterium tuberculosis* lurked around all those millennia, held off by good living conditions until large towns and less well-balanced diets at A.D. 1000 permitted it to rage.

An alternate hypothesis draws a parallel with post-Columbian epidemics in the Americas introduced by European and African immigrants. (African slaves were brought to America soon after Spanish conquests.) American Indians lacking prior exposure to diseases common in immigrants' homelands were devastated by epidemics. These epidemics were especially deadly because every-one in the community got sick and there was nobody to nurse them, bring water, cook food, or get firewood to keep them warm. Unlike historic smallpox and the Black Death (bubonic plague), tuberculo-sis epidemics don't kill off two-thirds or more of a community within a couple of weeks or spread like wildfire. The parallel lies in the potential for immigrant carriers from populations where tuberculo-sis was endemic for generations to infect native people in a port, who then go inland, get sick, and infect communities who never were near a European. These in turn infect more, sometimes as ref-ugees fleeing a sick town. It is firmly documented that in the Amer-icas, smallpox traveled well ahead of Europeans in the sixteenth, seventeenth, and eighteenth centuries, depopulating countrysides decades before the first European visits.

Using the model of historic epidemics, we can postulate that Norse in the Gulf of St. Lawrence infected American Indians, who then carried *Mycobacterium tuberculosis* upriver, through the Great Lakes and Mississippi Valley. Icelandic sagas written two or more centuries after L'Anse aux Meadows describe very limited trading between Norse and "Skraelings," but it could be that men who came for timber were friendly with local people, even perhaps persuading fair maidens to favor them for a night. Tuberculosis was endemic in Scandinavia, and well-fed men could carry the bac-terium without succumbing to illness. St. Lawrence Valley Indi-ans wintered in small, heavily insulated houses ideal for disseminating *Mycobacterium tuberculosis*. Visiting traders and relatives slept with host families in these houses. The disease would disproportionately hit larger towns where most of the people ate a lot of corn and not as much variety of other foods as nutritionists recommend. The combination of towns with relatively dense housing, furnishing a large pool for the bacteria to infect, and poorly balanced diets would make Mississippian populations in the Midwest vulnerable to an introduced epidemic. It is striking how close to A.D. 1000 the majority of the dated instances of tubercular-type lesions in American Indian cemeteries are.

Does the geographic range of these sites, from Peru to the American Southwest and Midwest, mean that *Mycobacterium tuberculosis* could not have been introduced by Europeans? The range does make it improbable that the disease was bovine tuberculosis caught from bison. Llamas, not bison, were Peruvians' domesticated animals; llamas can catch tuberculosis from humans, and if this happened, llama herds might have become reservoirs of tuberculosis. Tuberculosis is recognized in Chinese populations from the Han period (206 B.C.) on, as well as in Japan and Hawai'i from the mid first millennium A.D. Thus it could have reached Peru via Polynesian explorers: Polynesians apparently did not colonize inhabited South America as they did uninhabited Pacific islands, but seafarers who found, and returned to settle, tiny Easter Island surely reached the South American continent (see Green 1998). Midwestern populations thousands of miles from western South America more likely were infected by Norse from the east.

Mississippian centers had trade networks running from the Gulf of Mexico to the St. Lawrence Valley, from the Atlantic and Appalachians to the Rockies. Via the Arkansas River, and also across Texas, later Mississippians traded directly with Pueblos. In the seventeenth and eighteenth centuries, Midwestern and Northern Plains Indians gave eyewitness descriptions of Spanish settlements in New Mexico to French explorers coming from Quebec. Pueblos, particularly those in Chaco Canyon in the eleventh century, traded with Mexico, exchanging New Mexican turquoise for live, brilliantly colored macaw parrots from southeastern Mexican jungles. West Mexico traded with Peru. All these long-distance trades required entrepreneurs to stay for weeks in foreign towns. The model of post-Columbian disease introductions can accommodate such a picture of rapid and extensive spread, and from widely separated initial exposures.

The possibility that tuberculosis in the Upper Midwest in the early Mississippian period, around A.D. 1000, spread from Norse in Vinland is not directly relevant to the issue of the Kensington Runestone. It does suggest more contact between Norse and American Indians than the Icelandic sagas record, and thus indirectly affects the probability of Norse far west of Vinland later than L'Anse aux Meadows, but well within the half-millennium of Norse settlements in Greenland and resource procurement in America.

"BLOND MANDAN"

A persistent story from the early post-Revolution United States claims the Mandan people of the Missouri River Valley in central North Dakota were "White" and spoke a non-Indian language, supposedly Welsh. A Prince Madoc of Wales was said to have sailed west with a boatload of his people in 1170. Why such a group would have made their colony thousands of miles inland isn't explained. Historian Roger G. Kennedy, a retired director of the Smithsonian's National Museum of American History, noted that in 1583, Queen Elizabeth I of Britain was told by one of her ministers that "Mutuzuma" (Motecuhzoma), Principal Lord of the Aztecs, spoke Welsh words to Cortés. By virtue of this "fact," she was advised, she could lay claim to all of America, because the words attested that her own Welsh forebears must have taken over America before Columbus. Elizabeth prudently did not press the claim. Kennedy lists other reports of Welsh-speaking Whites from Alabama and South Carolina but always "just over the western horizon," Kennedy remarks (1994:233).

In 1950, Smithsonian biological anthropologist Marshall Newman published a review of the "blond Mandan" accounts, lamenting that severe decimation of the nation by nineteenth-century smallpox epidemics and the consequent amalgamation of the survivors with those from allied Missouri Valley farming towns left too few Mandan for any twentieth-century determination of pre-conquest physical characteristics. Newman's review concluded that there seems to have been a genetic tendency in some Mandan families for gray or gray-streaked hair even in early childhood (technically termed achromotrichia). This genetic trait was reported by European explorers and traders in other Northern Plains nations as well.

A second factor was a belief among Mandan and Hidatsa, a related nation just north of Mandan, that a young man might gain spiritual power from an older, successful man through first the older man, then the younger man, having intercourse with the same woman. The woman would be a channel through whom power would pass. Traditionally, this was carried out as a ritual in which the older man was considered to be like a bison bull, protecting the cows and young with his power. When fur traders showed up in Mandan and Hidatsa towns, their self-confidence, weapons, and wealth of goods labeled them men of power. Ambitious young men brought their wives to the traders, petitioning them to sleep with the women. European, French-Canadian, and American men were only too happy to oblige, marveling that the young women did not ask for presents. Word got around fast that Mandan and Hidatsa towns were ideal for wintering, offering warm, roomy earth-lodges; plenty of stored corn and dried meat; and a fresh young woman, free, nearly every night. Only the young husbands could testify whether they gained spiritual power from following up, but we can suppose that a likely concrete result from the power transfer would be, nine months later, a baby less Indian-looking than its Mandan or Hidatsa social father.

Contributing to the story that Mandan were lighter-skinned and some had brown hair rather than black was their style of living. Both Mandan and Hidatsa were agricultural, raising corn, beans, squashes, and tobacco in river valley fields. They produced considerable surpluses to trade for meat, hides, tools, and ornaments with nomadic nations of the Plains grasslands, making their permanent, fortified riverside towns the market towns of the Northern Plains. Their homes were commodious constructions of wooden frames covered with thick blocks of sod, cool in summer and warm in winter. People worked and socialized inside their houses rather than in the open as with nomadic tipi-dwellers. Therefore, Mandan and Hidatsa tended to be less tanned and weathered than nomads. They hunted and labored in the fields, but families might buy slaves to do drudgery while young ladies embroidered trousseaus. Sacajawea, Lewis and Clark's young Shoshone guide, was such a slave, bought by the French-Canadian trader Charbonneau to be his concubine and assist his two wives. Lewis and Clark and their Corps of Discovery chose to winter over in a Mandan town.

Hjalmar Holand suggested that "blond Mandans" represented Paul Knutson's evangelical expedition seeking fallen-away Norse Greenlander Christians. Holand thought Knutson, like Lewis and Clark, would have settled with Mandan until spring allowed him to continue west, to Kensington he supposed. Knutson would have been fervent indeed to paddle thousands of miles inland searching for the apostates; Holand's hypothesis of a Knutson expedition seems only slightly less speculative than the legend of Prince Madoc.

Holand quotes an account by Swedish naturalist Peter (Pehr) Kalm, published in 1753–1761, of a conversation in Quebec in 1749 with "Mr. de Verandriere," surely Pierre Gaultier de Varennes, Sieur de la Vérendrye. Kalm said La Vérendrye described seeing, in Mandan country in central or eastern North Dakota, a pillar-like stone with a smaller stone fixed into it, the smaller one covered with writing unfamiliar to him. According to Kalm, La Vérendrye removed the smaller stone, brought it back to Montreal, and sent it to the French Secretary of State. Holand thought the unfamiliar writing was probably runes. On his trip to France in 1911 with the Kensington Runestone, he spent some days in Paris searching museums there, in vain, for the Vérendrye stone. Two archaeologists who analyzed La Vérendrye's and his sons' rather scanty published accounts of their explorations in the Northern Plains (1738–1743), do not mention Peter Kalm's story, but do note that an inscribed lead tablet placed by the sons near Fort Pierre, South Dakota, in 1743, was recovered in 1913. It was on a hill overlooking the Missouri River; on one side was a stamped Latin inscription serving to proclaim French sovereignty, on the other the inscribed names of the Chevalier de la Vérendrye and two of his men, "30 March 1743." Possibly Kalm confused mention of the claim to sovereignty with discovery of an inscribed tablet.

The senior La Vérendrye remarked, upon reaching a Mandan town in 1738, "I admit that I was surprised, having expected to see a people different from other Indians, especially in view of the account we had been given. They [Mandans] are not at all different from the Assiniboins . . . I knew by this time that we would have to discount everything we had been told about them" (Smith 1980:51). The Vérendryes themselves realized that Indian acquaintances' descriptions of white-skinned people were of Spanish colonists, objects of curiosity and sources of booty for raiding Plains troops. Anthropologist Marshall Newman concluded that the Mandan were not unlike other Northern Plains Indians, nor have linguists found any Welsh words in the Mandan language. Their ritual of young wives "walking with the buffaloes" to enhance their husbands' spiritual power undoubtedly added European genes to the Mandan population, beginning early in the eighteenth century, several generations before visits by Prince Maximilian of Wied and by George Catlin, two observers who wrote in detail on Mandan towns. The scientific principle "Occam's Razor," to slash away elaborate interpretations until one has a minimum of factors sufficient to explain a phenomenon, tells us that early Norse or Welsh are not needed to account for Mandan appearance: it suffices to list unremarkable variations in hair, eye, and skin color; skin less deeply tanned among people living in large permanent houses; and admixture of genes from traders willing to oblige young couples seeking transfer of power.

RED HORN AND RED-HAIRED GIANTS

The Gottschall Rock Shelter (named after the landowner) in southwest Wisconsin is a shallow cave at the head of a ravine leading to the Wisconsin River. The rock shelter's acoustics make speech at the back seem to come from its opening, so it is difficult to correctly locate sounds within the rock shelter. Perhaps this odd feature made ancient visitors think it might harbor a holy presence. The shelter had been used intermittently since about 1500 B.C., then starting about 600 B.C., rituals were held in it, indicated to the archaeologist by layers of burned sections and overlays of a mixture of ash, burned and ground limestone, and ground bone and clamshell. About A.D. 1000—since the dates are determined from radiocarbon dating, a true calendar date would be in the range A.D. 900–1100—a mural was painted on the back wall of the shelter. It portrays a scene recognized by Ho-Chunk as featuring their hero Red Horn accompanied by his comrades Turtle and the thunderbird Storms-As-He-Walks. Down in a lower corner of the mural is a small man smoking a pipe, perhaps a priest invoking the legend. Red Horn is more than mortal; in the mural, he wears a disc with radiating lines on top of his forehead, likely indicating his status as the morning star manifesting in human form. Also called "He Who Wears Human Heads for Pendants," he has a pair of little heads at his nipples that stick out their tongues at the enemy at one point in the story. The painting shows Red Horn with tattoos on his chest and arms as was customary for men (their "mark of honor") among the Siouan-speaking nations of the Midwest, such as the Ho-Chunk.

Two giants, twice the size of Red Horn, confront him in the mural. Storms-As-He-Walks, as big as the giants, stands between them and Red Horn, while Turtle is above them. The giants wear star- or sun-like discs on their foreheads, like Red Horn's, but they are not tattooed. The giant on the left has no clothing unless stippling at the bottom of the torso and on the thighs is meant to be leggings. The right-hand giant has a plain oval on its chest and an apron-like garment with lines on it that look like woven or embroidered cloth. This giant has no legs; the other's legs are curtailed at mid-thigh. The right-hand giant is not as large as its companion, and it has red-painted hair with a blue feather in it and a small upside-down animal, possibly a bird, hanging from the end of its long forelock. At the end of its left hand, in front of Storms-As-He-Walks, is a mess of lines that seem to have been painted over whatever was originally drawn. According to the legend, giants challenged the Indian people. First, Red Horn and his comrades persuaded the giants to meet them on the playing field, contesting

Painted panel at the Gottschall Rockshelter, Wisconsin, Late Prehistoric period. Hochungara (Ho-Chunk, Winnebago) viewing the panel believe it to represent the story of their ancient hero Red Horn, shown battling giants as a thunderbird watches. Above the giants is a turtle. Reprinted by permission of the Wisconsin Archeological Society.

them in lacrosse. A female giant with red hair led her team, but between Storms-As-He-Walks launching thunder when she came near him and Red Horn's little heads sticking out their tongues and winking when she approached, making her laugh, the giant team lost the ball game. Storms-As-He-Walks killed all the giants except the red-haired woman, who married Red Horn. Ho-Chunk today see the red-haired giant, in the center of the panel, to be this woman.

Robert Salzer, an archaeologist who has been excavating Gottschall and consulting with Ho-Chunk, believes the Red Horn mural may represent a historical event, as Ho-Chunk aver. Salzer points to the construction of Aztalan, a fortified Wisconsin outpost, and sites along the Mississippi as far north as Trempeleau, west of Gottschall, as evidencing ties to the prehistoric state of Cahokia (centered in what is now St. Louis). The simplest explanation, keeping with the principle of Occam's Razor, is to premise that Ho-Chunk forebears battled invading Cahokians. But if Norse went inland when they built L'Anse aux Meadows, it would be equally simple to premise that they were the invaders in Wisconsin. Cahokians were no different physically from Ho-Chunk. Norse might have looked like red-haired giants to Wisconsin Indians. They could have learned to play lacrosse, and Norse women such as Freydis, Eirik's daughter, were fearless leaders. We can readily imagine Freydis leading her team, cracking up with laughter when Red Horn's little faces wiggled, and when the battle got serious, accepting to be his wife in exchange for her life being spared.

Yes, this scenario is speculation. That the painting of the mural took place approximately (radiocarbon dates are always approximate) when an epidemic of tuberculosis hit the Midwest and when Norse are definitively evidenced living at the Gulf of St. Lawrence correlates three independent sets of data logically leading to a plausible scenario. The Ho-Chunk legend says Red Horn's people burned the bodies of the giants they killed; we cannot recover skeletons to confirm, or disprove, the scenario.

CONCLUSION

Biological anthropology is of tangential usefulness in evaluating the probability that the Kensington Runestone is authentic. Eighteenth-century rumors that blond Indians lived in the West need to be discussed because several writers attribute the supposed blond nation to Welsh or Norse colonizing. Mandan hospitality to visitors, including fur traders, brought in European genes that added to the natural range of hair, eye, and skin color in Northern Plains Indians. The A.D. 1000 tuberculosis epidemic occurred three-and-a-half centuries before the Runestone's date of 1362 but hints at earlier Norse penetrations into the American interior, although the disease could have been passed inland via other Indians from Norse at the Gulf of St. Lawrence as well. Gottschall's Red Horn mural is least significant, because the legend it probably illustrates says no more than that the hero's enemies were red-haired giants; Red Horn himself is said to have had red hair, reducing the distinction between him and his opponents. Considering whether the mural might show Norse in conflict with Ho-Chunk is a "thought experiment," thinking through a logical outcome *if* there were Norse–Ho-Chunk encounters.

Chapter Seven

The Norse

Contrary to popular belief, there were no Vikings in Scandinavia in the fourteenth century. The term "Viking" belongs to Scandinavians between about A.D. 760 to 1080, when the last kingdom accepted Christianity. Church bishops answering to the Pope in Rome had shared political power with kings and barons for two and a half centuries by 1362. A legacy from the Viking Age was a set of trade routes stretching enormous distances both east and west—east up through Finland and northern Russia, down the Dnieper River to the Black Sea and across it to Constantinople (Istanbul) and even farther east into Asia, west by sea past Iceland and Greenland to the Canadian Arctic and Labrador.

Scandinavia was in crisis in the mid-fourteenth century. The Black Death (bubonic plague) hit in 1349, scourging the population for a decade and rapidly killing half the population of Sweden and one-third of Norway (whose population was more rural and dispersed). Radical depopulation hit kings and aristocrats in the pocketbook, depressing rents as much of the best farmland lost tenants and the state lost taxes. A coalition of neighboring German merchants, the Hanse, took advantage of societal disruption to consolidate economic power. About 1350, they established a permanent community of Germans in Norway's best port, Bergen; by 1360, there were some 3000 German men in Bergen, governing themselves, forbidden to socialize or intermarry with Norwegians, and using violence to maintain their dominance. At this time, the Hanse began using gunpowder. They took over both inland and coastal retail trade, subordinating Norwegians, and controlled the lucrative stockfish (dried cod) export out of Bergen. The Hanse also dominated Scandinavia's other great fishery, salted herring from the Öresund off Sweden, by controlling the import of salt mined from near Lübeck.

The Hanse had developed in the 1100s from merchants traveling together in bands for protection. Lübeck, on the Baltic in present Schleswig-Holstein on the German border, was founded in 1159 as a free city by west-German merchants using newly developed cogs (cargo sailing ships with one or two masts, not dependent on oars). Two years later, German Hanse took advantage of a treaty between Saxony and Gotland to form a community in Visby on Gotland Island. The Hanse was not a coalition of states, nor was it, like contemporary Italian merchant societies, a business corporation. Its merchants had capital, the best cargo ships and port facilities, and privileges obtained through their organized economic power. They profited from exporting Scandinavian iron and copper, timber, goat- and sheepskins, lamp oil from cod and sea mammals, walrus ivory and hides, and furs. Furs were mostly transshipped, some from the Greenland Norse via Bergen and most, mainly northern gray squirrel, from Russia. Hanse imported rye from German farms on the Baltic and cloth from England, as well as salt, into Scandinavia; exports were nearly twice as great as imports, with profits going to the Hanse.

In 1362, Magnus Eiriksson was King of Sweden. He had been born in 1316 to Prince Eirik of Sweden and Ingebjørg, daughter of Haakon V, King of Norway. Haakon V died in 1319, leaving little Magnus, living in Sweden with Ingebjørg, heir to the Norwegian throne. Ingebjørg and the Swedish royal council negotiated a union between Sweden and Norway, making Magnus Eiriksson king of both Norway and Sweden and Ingebjørg and the two kingdoms' councils regent for the boy king. In 1332, teenage Magnus came of age. That year, he agreed to a request by the nobility of the Danish provinces Skåne and Blekinge to be their king: King Kristoffer II of Denmark had turned these provinces over to Count Johan of Holstein in payment of his debt to Johan. Magnus paid Johan what Kristoffer owed him, 34,000 silver marks (something like 3 million dollars). In 1335, Magnus married Blanca of Namur, who brought as dowry the provinces Ranafylke and Borgarsyssel, plus Iceland;

Magnus' morning gift to Blanca was several southern Norwegian fiefs including Vestfold. St. Birgitta of Sweden was mistress of robes to Queen Blanca.

Magnus, nicknamed Magnus Smek (pronounced "Smaake"; *smeka* is Swedish for "fondle, caress") and Blanca had two sons, the younger, born in 1340, named Haakon. In 1342, Norway and Sweden, both ruled by Magnus, battled King Valdemar (IV) Atterdag of Denmark, who wanted Skåne back. The German Hanse allied with Valdemar. Valdemar lost in 1343 and ceded Skåne and other territory to Magnus for 49,000 marks (about 4 million dollars) but Magnus had to borrow the money from the Hanseatic Germans. In return, he had to grant or confirm their trading and tax-exemption privileges. At the same time, Norwegian barons demanded separation from Sweden, with the boy Haakon to be their king when he came of age in 1355.

Valdemar of Denmark invaded and seized Helsingborg, Skåne, and Blekinge in Sweden in 1359, and in 1361 took the islands Öland and Gotland and sacked Visby on Gotland. That year, the Hanse unsuccessfully allied with Norway and Sweden against Valdemar, then in 1362 turned against Norway and Sweden. Haakon had quarreled with his father Magnus and imprisoned him briefly, until negotiations made Haakon king of Sweden jointly with Magnus. Finally, in 1363 Haakon married Valdemar's ten-year-old daughter Margaret, who became heir to the Danish throne two months later when her brother died. Scandinavia's three kingdoms were now allied. By 1366, the Hanse began complaining that Norway and Denmark were not allowing the German merchants their full privileges, and the next year, 1367, the Hanseatic League was formally organized in Cologne as a coalition of towns, with merchants from a particular town represented as a group, not individuals, in the Hanse Diet (parliament). The League allied in 1368 with Norway, Sweden, and Mecklenburg (Germany) against Denmark; this war concluded in 1370 with Denmark the loser.

THE FUR TRADE

Norway and much of Sweden are mountainous, forested, cold, and poor for farming. While fishing and hunting helped sustain the population, natural increase drove thousands beyond Scandinavia. The

Viking Age is named after the Norse word for piracy, when Norse used their fast sailing ships to raid coastal farms and towns throughout western Europe. Conversion to Christianity brought Scandinavia into political and trade relations involving the Pope and his bishops appointed to dioceses throughout Scandinavia, including Iceland and Greenland. Although church tithes had to be paid, kings could borrow money from church officials and work through or with them to open and protect international trade. In part because medieval Christendom fostered long-distance trade, markets, and credit, demand grew for luxuries such as ivory and beautiful furs.

Even though Scandinavia's agricultural output was limited, it did have walruses with ivory tusks and valuable fur animals in its north. Demand was fed by laws declaring certain furs exclusive to royalty, others to the aristocracy: *vair*,[1] skins of long-haired gray squirrels trapped in northern Russia, was especially desired to line cloaks and trim garments. Scandinavian men consolidated the fur trade by conquering and colonizing the gray squirrels' land and building market centers on the Dnieper and the Volga. With Kiev and Novgorod their principal towns, they were called the Rus; Russia is named for them. Rus noblemen, called boyars, collected squirrel and ermine skins from their peasant tenants and paid these as taxes to their princes at Novgorod and Kiev. There, the furs were packed into barrels and shipped downriver to Constantinople and other eastern cities, or north and west through headwaters and marshes to the Baltic and western Europe. Slaves carried boats and goods through portages, and slave women were kept for sex and domestic work. The months-long trips were difficult and dangerous, and brothers and comrades of Norse who died en route often erected memorial stones to them back home in Scandinavia. There, back home, successful traders paid taxes to their kings.

By the early fourteenth century, an expanding middle class in Europe challenged the status symbols of aristocracy. Rich merchants bought Russian squirrel-lined cloaks and prices fell. Less common furs—ermine, sable, and beaver—became signs of high status. These, too, could come from Russia, but unlike *vair*, they also could be trapped in northern America. Greenlandic Norse hunted these furs, traded for them with Inuit, and sold them and walrus ivory and hides to pay their taxes and buy imports from Norway and beyond. When the Hanse took over Bergen in the mid-fourteenth century,

Scandinavians had long been familiar with American furs. Norse could not contend with the Hanse stranglehold around the Baltic, cutting them off from Russia, but the Hanse were not equipped to explore far-distant, unorganized sources of furs. After 1370, the Hanse slowly lost power until, reduced to nine towns, it ceased at just the time the Hudson's Bay Company was chartered, 1670.

The idea of Norse from Scandinavia or Greenland going inland all the way to western Minnesota is less amazing when one looks at a map of Europe and sees how far, and through what wilderness, Norse had been journeying to Byzantium for centuries. Northern American Indians of the fourteenth century would not have seemed much different from Saami in northern Scandinavia and Finland or the "wild tribes" Rus had to deal with in Russia. Throughout the subarctic zone, in America as in Eurasia, native inhabitants lived by hunting and fishing, moving camp seasonally, and preparing animal skins for their own clothing and bedding and to trade for products of temperate lands to their south. Traversing the network of streams and swamps between Finland and the Volga, Norse traders might leave their boats, portage goods overland through forest for several days, then have their men build new boats for the eastern river system. It should not have fazed men experienced in the eastern fur trade to sail up the St. Lawrence through the Great Lakes to Duluth at the western end of Lake Superior and paddle in Indian canoes to the Kensington area. Alternately, they could have boated through Hudson Strait and Hudson Bay to the mouths of the Nelson or Hayes Rivers in Manitoba, up either river to Lake Winnipeg, down the Red River, and so on to northwestern Minnesota. Leaving lake-going boats at Duluth, traveling in canoes to Kensington would take about fourteen days, or by the alternate route, they could have left their boats at Winnipeg, a similar distance to Kensington. Indian guides could have been hired, as they have been throughout historic centuries, and their advice weighed against the Norse traders' experience in reading northern landscapes.

It is significant that the Kensington Runestone states its party was composed of Goths and Norwegians, not Greenlanders. Goths and Norwegians were familiar with forest habitats of ermine, sable, and beaver. Greenlandic Norse traded and themselves hunted in the Arctic and Labrador for walrus, arctic fox, polar bears, and white falcons. Greenlanders may have hunted in the forested part of Labrador or, more likely, obtained furs trapped by Indians and brought to coastal trading fairs; they had no particular incentive to explore far inland. In 1362, Goths and Norwegians cut off from the lucrative Russian fur trade did have incentive to explore comparable lands on the western edge of the Norse economic sphere.

Considering the geography of northwestern Minnesota, ethnohistorian Helen Hornbeck Tanner notices that Kensington is on an upland from which flow the headwaters of rivers leading to three major water routes: the Minnesota, Red, and Mississippi Rivers. The area is on the border between the northeastern plains and woodlands, the southwestern limit of wild rice, and an eastern zone for bison herds. Tanner, deeply knowledgeable from preparing her lauded *Atlas of Great Lakes Indian History* (1987), suggests that the party of Goths and Norwegians may have considered building a trading post on the Kensington-area upland to facilitate collecting furs from Indian trappers. Finding ten of their party "red with blood and dead" would have been a setback, but not unfamiliar to men with experience in the Byzantium trade. On that long route, it had been feasible to bring along enough men to construct Norse trading centers at Kiev and Novgorod and to ally with kings and the Byzantine emperor to convoy traders under armed guards. Our party of Goths and Norwegians at Kensington must have been acutely aware that the ocean between America and Scandinavia cut them off from ready reinforcements; like historic fur traders in Canada, survival depended upon friendly relations with the indigenous nations.

Compared to that historic fur trade, fourteenth-century Norse were undercapitalized and lacked the patronage of imperialist states. As the foregoing review of Scandinavian history indicates, medieval kingdoms were unstable, with rulers vying and conspiring, borrowing heavily and forced to concede large territories to their debtors, not to mention marrying ten-year-old girls to make a political alliance. Drastic population losses from the Black Death exacerbated the kingdoms' fiscal crises. In contrast, by 1670 when the Hudson's Bay Company was established, England had a strong central state built a century earlier by the Tudors Henry VIII and Elizabeth I, a large population with increasingly well-managed farms spinning off laborers seeking employment in cities or on ships, and an upper class looking to mercantile investments, rather than piracy, to increase their wealth. Prince Rupert, a duke, three earls, and other nobles subscribed to the Company of Adventurers of England Trading Into Hudson's Bay, proposed by two Canadian-born Frenchmen to circumvent the French government monopoly on the Canadian fur trade channeled through St. Lawrence Valley depots. Start-up and operating expenses were so great it took fourteen years before the Hudson's Bay Company earned enough to pay dividends to its investors. Similar to England in 1670, France had a centralized state headed by Louis XIV, the "Sun King," sponsoring and investing in international enterprises designed to heighten its military and political as well as economic power. The difference between 1362 and 1670 was the difference between medieval and modern economies. The Goths and Norwegians at Kensington might have created a sustainable fur trade, but constraints on capital and patronage would have kept them well below the power and profit of the Hudson's Bay Company.

What initially brought the North Atlantic to world importance was not furs, but codfish. Dried cod was a staple protein in medieval Europe. Northern Norway was a major producer, having both cod in its waters and a cool climate allowing air-drying of the fish. As European population increased and the church, in league with governments, imposed more meatless fast days, demand rose for salted or dried cod. In the fifteenth century, fishing fleets from all the Atlantic coastal nations converged on Iceland and, by the 1480s, farther west on the cod-rich Newfoundland Banks. Early in the sixteenth century, hundreds of sailing vessels anchored in Canadian coastal waters every summer while crews caught and processed tons of fish, most of the preparation done in camps on shore. Indians came to the coast to trade furs for European items the crews brought along for small-scale private trading. Exploitation of the Newfoundland Banks, and presumably processing on Canadian shores, was established before Columbus involved Spain in tropical America. Historical documentation is limited, in part because merchants financing fishing fleets guarded business secrets from competitors. We cannot yet determine to what degree five centuries of Norse, particularly Greenlandic Norse, utilization of Canada's timber, fish, game, and Indian and Inuit trade laid the foundation for sixteenth-century commercial development of the North Atlantic.

ANOTHER DIMENSION

The principle of Occam's Razor—taught by medieval English philosopher William of Ockham—is that one should not burden a scientific claim with unnecessary items ("Entities should not be multiplied unnecessarily"). That is, one should slash away ideas and facts not critical to one's argument. Following Occam's principle, this chapter has not described the intellectual culture of fourteenth-century Scandinavia: political and economic events are sufficient to suggest that it was reasonable for a group of Norwegians and Götlanders to travel west of Vinland in 1362 to acquire something, most probably furs.

It is possible that at least one man on the expedition hoped to acquire a most precious object, the legendary Holy Grail. On the first four lines of the Kensington Runestone inscription, six letters carry additional marking, verified by Wolter's examination to have been deliberately cut. These six letters spell "gral ăr," translated as "grail is." The legend that the blood of the crucified Jesus had been caught in a bowl (medieval French *grail*) and was preserved somewhere, presumably in western Asia, was popular in fourteenth-century Europe. Götland was a center for the Teutonic Knights, who were allied with the Knights Templar, an organization of knights dedicated to protecting Christians in Jerusalem and on the Crusades. Götland also had establishments of the widespread Cistercian Order of monks. The man who composed the text of the Kensington Runestone clearly was formally educated, likely in a school run by monks, and would have known the legend of the miraculous Grail. He would have seen world maps that in his time, and even in Columbus's day a century and a half later, depicted a single land mass surrounded by a world ocean. Like Columbus, he could have figured that by traveling west from Europe, he would cross the world ocean to the eastern side of the landmass, that is, Asia, and might find the wondrous Grail.

It is intriguing to consider what that literate Götlander might have been thinking as he tramped with his comrades through forests and prairies he had been taught had to be in Asia. But a quest, or even simple hope, to discover the Holy Grail isn't necessary as motivation for the expedition that memorialized ten dead in Minnesota. Well-documented political and economic events in mid-fourteenth-century Scandinavia adequately account for the expedition.

Note

[1] Cinderella's slippers were made of *vair*, that is, they were luxuriously soft, warm squirrel fur. An English translator mistakenly thought the French original word was *verre*, "glass."

Chapter Eight

On the American Side

In contrast with the well-documented European case, the history of the Kensington region during the fourteenth century has to be constructed on archaeological data correlated with ethnographic and ethnohistorical records. Since neither impressive sites nor well-funded cultural-resource management projects occur in the region, its archaeology has been limited, and little has been published. Pale though the archaeological picture appears, it does show indigenous populations skilled in hunting and accustomed to trade over long distances.

Minnesota's State Archaeological Survey divides the state into eight regions. Interestingly, Kensington is on the southwestern boundary of the Central Deciduous [Forest] Lakes, abutting the Prairie Lake and Red River Valley regions; in other words, it is well positioned to reach resources of the forested zone with deer and numerous lakes bearing wild rice and fish, the prairie zone with bison, and corn-growing settlements to the south. It was poor country for immigrant farmers from Europe but desirable for Indians living by a seasonal round harvesting native foods. This type of economy did not support dense populations, hence the landscape looked wild, with little groups of tents or wigwams leaving only scattered traces of habitation.

Archaeologist Guy Gibbon proposed the name Psinomani, a Dakota word for "wild rice gatherer," for the culture pattern observable in most of Minnesota by the fourteenth century. Psinomani

71

probably included ancestors of the historic Dakota. As Gibbon's term implies, Psinomani cultivated, gathered, and processed wild rice as a staple of their subsistence; roots, tubers, berries, and nuts also were harvested. Deer and fish were important, as were seasonal bison-hunting excursions. People probably lived in small villages of round, bark-covered wigwams, using hide tents on extended hunts. Clothing was likely sewn using soft-tanned buckskin, with bison robes for winter outerwear and bedding. Women wove a variety of baskets and flexible bags and manufactured clay cooking pots. Men carved wooden bowls and made stone-tipped arrows, spears, and bows. Both women and men made nets and snared small game. Social organization stressed cooperation balanced by respect for individuals' judgment, an ethos that let people travel and shift residence to another band if they preferred. Some communities constructed modest burial mounds for their leaders.

Historically, American Indians often were multilingual so as to facilitate extended visiting and trade; this likely was common in the fourteenth century, too. Trade moved catlinite pipestone from southwestern Minnesota, chert for knives and arrowheads from the Knife River of central North Dakota, copper from Lake Superior, and bits of obsidian from northern Wyoming into northwestern Minnesota. Transcontinental trade links are visible in finds of Pacific Northwest dentalium shells and Gulf of Mexico conch. Judging from amounts of non-local materials in sites, trade seems to have increased in the fourteenth century. Historically, there were Indian trade fairs on the James River of southeastern North Dakota and at Lake Traverse sixty miles west of Kensington on the Dakota border.

Marked changes are manifest in archaeological data from the mid-fourteenth century. People moved into larger villages, and many were strongly fortified with log palisades and ditches. One, the Crow Creek site in central South Dakota, had over fifty earthlodge homes inside its bastioned, ditched fortification, unfortunately overcome by attackers who massacred nearly five hundred inhabitants. An archaeological culture (that is, artifact style, settlement pattern, and economy) termed Oneota spread westward from Wisconsin from the tenth century through the fourteenth. Oneota were farmers who raised maize (corn), beans, squashes, and sunflowers (for edible seeds) and traveled west each year to hunt bison, bringing back dried meat. In contrast to their western neighbors on the northeastern plains, Oneota large villages were not fortified;

why so many communities over the Upper Midwest felt so secure, we do not know.

Norse entering into northwestern Minnesota in 1362, whether from the north or the east, would have moved through the peripheries of Oneota, too far north for maize to be grown but where pottery style and other artifacts resemble Oneota. Indians resident in northern Minnesota were very probably ancestors of the Dakota (and Assinboin, who had split from the Dakota by the seventeenth century). Annual excursions to hunt bison, along with the many entrepreneurs traveling to trade, gave Minnesota Dakota familiarity with agricultural Oneota south of them, who were ancestral to the Ioway, Oto, and other midwestern Siouans, and to the Cheyenne, Mandan, and Hidatsa to the west. Thus Kensington was not only on an ecological border, it was on a political frontier. Who left the ten men "red with blood and dead"? Dakota resenting intrusion into their domain? Oneota Siouans or Cheyenne warning them not to invade their farmlands?

WAS THERE A FUR TRADE IN THE FOURTEENTH CENTURY?

Whether Minnesota's fourteenth-century increase in trade and warfare might reflect Norse involvement is an intriguing question. If this might be so, then the European fur trade began two centuries earlier than documented, other than that between Greenlandic Norse and Inuit. Not until England and France developed capital and strong governments promoting imperial outreach did the American fur trade gain historic notice. It also happened that beaver became a lucrative commodity in the late seventeenth and throughout the eighteenth century due to fashions utilizing beaver-hair felt for hats. Beaver are more numerous and much easier to catch than marten (sable) and weasel (ermine), the fur-bearers most prized in the late medieval period. The beaver trade rewarded capital investment in manpower, posts, and transport more readily than less-numerous, elusive, and sly ermines and sables.

To assess the possibility of Norse attempting to trade along the woodlands/plains frontier, we should look at early historic trade between Europeans and Indians. The fourteenth century generally was a period of political changes: fallout from the collapse of

Cahokia, the only real state in the pre-European United States. Filling the rich floodplain where the Missouri River flows into the Mississippi (present-day St. Louis), Cahokia spread out from a huge plaza surrounded by earthen pyramids, the most awesome one hundred feet high with a flat top larger than a football field. Other plazas with pyramid mounds lay over the river plain, probably serving segments of the city population. Intensively cultivated maize fields fed the city. Cahokia's power seems to have covered the heart of the Midwest, from southern Wisconsin to Arkansas. How it gained its power, how it operated during the somewhat less than two centuries of its heyday, we cannot discern from the archaeology; a reasonable guess is that it trafficked in perishables, possibly selling maize, velvety tanned deerskins, and slaves downriver to Mexican markets. Cahokia's rise and collapse coincided with the rise and collapse of the Toltec state in Mexico, forerunner of the Aztecs. (So did the Southwest's most impressive site, the cluster of grand pueblos in Chaco Canyon, New Mexico.) Oneota developed at the same time as Cahokia, only its more northern situation limited its maize production so that it did not support populations dense enough to build impressive capital cities. After Cahokia collapsed, Oneota spread over much of its territory.

At historic contact, late seventeenth century, the Cahokia region was a frontier. Who had commanded the central Mississippi Valley more than four centuries earlier cannot be determined. A plausible hypothesis is that it had been the ancestors of the midwestern Siouans, perhaps the Osage, who were a major Midwest power in the early historic period and held a fertile and defensible plateau in Missouri upriver from Cahokia. Omaha, Kansa, Ponca, and Quapaw are closely related to Osage, historically occupying country west of the Mississippi from Arkansas and eastern Kansas and Nebraska through Missouri. Another series of Siouan speakers, the Ioway, Oto, Missouri, and Ho-Chunk, held the country to the north—Iowa, northern Missouri, southern Minnesota, and Wisconsin. Northwest of Ho-Chunk, Dakota occupied most of Minnesota, with Anishinaabe (Ojibwa) in the northeast and Cree north of Lake Superior.

More than a century of mediated trade preceded recorded European explorations in the northern Midwest. During this sixteenth-century protohistoric period, European artifacts appeared in many Indian communities. Small metal hawk bells were a popular import from the Spanish in Florida and the Coronado and de Soto expeditions to southern Kansas and Arkansas, respectively. In the east, pieces cut from iron-banded copper kettles brought by Basque whalers to processing stations at the Strait of Belle Isle (the L'Anse aux Meadows region at the narrows of the Gulf of St. Lawrence) and to the St. Lawrence estuary have been recovered from Indian sites around Lake Ontario and even in the Ohio River Valley at the West Virginia–Ohio border. On the Niagara frontier in western New York, a protohistoric Iroquois old man's grave contained a pottery imitation of a Basque kettle, hundreds of glass beads, and a metal model canoe! A pair of heavily fortified Huron Iroquois villages watched over a winding portage connecting Lake Ontario with Georgian Bay of Lake Huron, profiting from transshipping fine knapping chert from west of Lake Ontario to Huronia to the north. From the beginning of the sixteenth century protohistoric, Basque, and other European items appeared here. Blue glass beads have been recovered in New York state, the Detroit area, West Virginia, the lower Ohio Valley, northern Alabama, and Oneota territory of northeastern Iowa. Serpents fashioned from copper or European brass occur in sites from the west end of Lake Ontario, along the upper Ohio, around Chicago, at the junction of southwestern Wisconsin, southeastern Minnesota, and northeastern Iowa, and farthest west, in northwesternmost Iowa. This last trail of artifacts indicates trade throughout Oneota country, while the previous artifacts trace trade by Iroquoians (which may include Huron and Neutral as well as New York and St. Lawrence Iroquois).

Minnesota's historic fur trade began in the seventeenth century with French efforts to expand beyond its seventeenth-century colonization of the St. Lawrence Valley. Along the St. Lawrence, French emigrants negotiated with indigenous Iroquoian nations, and Iroquois men were integral to French trading ventures and to independent Anglo enterprises. Iroquois economies were based on women carrying on agriculture around their villages while most of the men traveled to hunt and trade, often hundreds or even thousands of miles. An Iroquois account of the Creator discovering a rival on the western rim of the world suggests Iroquois were familiar with the Rocky Mountains in Montana, which may have stimulated two groups of Iroquois to escape United States domination by settling along the Rockies, in Montana and Alberta, early in the nineteenth century. To get there, they would have traversed the

Great Lakes and Manitoba to the Saskatchewan River, the major fur trader route for French and independents. If Iroquoian long-distance trading goes back to the fourteenth century, they could have guided Norse from the Gulf of St. Lawrence far inland along the river and through the Great Lakes. If, alternately, the Norse sailed into Hudson Bay and canoed along the Hudson's Bay Company route, they would have used Cree guides as did the first Bay inland explorer, Henry Kelsey, in 1690. Kelsey's Cree companions were not focused much on trade, in contrast to seventeenth-century Iroquois.

Could there have been a Norse fur trade in inland America in the fourteenth century? There *could* have been, considering American Indians had been trading across the continent for millennia. Feasible routes for canoe transport were well known; guides, translators, and porters were available, and towns selling food and hosting trading fairs were established at key points. The St. Lawrence–Great Lakes route, which began in Iroquoia, left larger boats at the west end of Lake Superior at Duluth, and continued about fourteen days farther west to Kensington, would have looked familiar to Scandinavians who had traversed their eastern fur trade route through northern Russia. The significant differences between 1362 and the late 1600s were, first, demands in Europe for American products that could be capitalized—produced in increasing quantities with increasing efficiency—and second, European states with capitalist economies and capability to support overseas ventures. Beaver in the north and finely tanned deerskins and tobacco in the south were commodities suited to late-seventeenth-century Europeans' search for investment opportunities.

Three centuries previously, medieval kingdoms could not command such capital. The expedition of Goths and Norwegians could have extended the poorly and privately financed, risky fur trade carried on by Greenlandic Norse, and possibly they did, but there was no Byzantium to anchor the far end of the route as in Europe. (Central Mexico had cities with huge markets, but trafficked in tropical products. Central Mexico was also very far from Norse in Canada, with trading routes traversing dozens of small kingdoms in the southern United States and then across the Gulf of Mexico to another series of kingdoms.) If our Goths and Norwegians got back to Scandinavia in 1363, the better bet for them would have been to join their kings in combating Hanse power to regain Scandinavia's former remunerative control over the Russian fur business.

A strong analogy to the possible 1362 effort at a fur trade occurred in 1581 when Sweden took the Baltic port of Narva, principal stopover for Russian furs traded into Europe. Basque entrepreneurs from southwestern France immediately took advantage of this disruption in the fur market to send ships to Canada specifically to bring back furs. For several decades previously, Basque whalers and cod fishermen had supplemented their catches with some furs traded from Gulf of St. Lawrence Indians. Now, a fortune could be made quickly: the captain of one of these trading ships sold his share of the voyage's cargo of furs for £3000. The bonanza didn't last. In 1585, Dutch merchants built a new trading depot at Archangel on the White Sea in Russia, and by 1587, Basques routed trading ships to Archangel rather than Canada. It is worth noting that information on the brief 1580s Basque shift to American furs was painstakingly winnowed out of French port notaries' records of transactions. Such data don't usually get into standard history books.

DOES THE KENSINGTON RUNESTONE REWRITE AMERICAN HISTORY?

Data and models at hand give us a choice of scenarios for Minnesota in 1362. Because the geologic evidence for weathering of the Runestone runes makes it probable that one party of Norse did reach Kensington, we can read the circumstances to infer that they were an anomaly: one expedition pushing far inland at a time of unique economic crisis in their homeland to find conditions for an American fur trade too dangerous and difficult to warrant persevering in the venture. Or, we can read the Runestone and archaeological data to suggest that Norse did persevere in attempting to break into existing Indian trade networks, escalating commerce and contributing to hostilities along the Midwest plains frontier. If an inland Norse fur trade did develop, it would have been so small in scale that it was soon subsumed into Greenlandic Norse exports. Either way, it does seem clear that American history as we know it will not be greatly altered by accepting the Kensington Runestone inscription.

That said, accepting the Runestone as authentic does affect our understanding of how American history has been constructed. Historians are trained to work from documents, primarily written records. This means our history conventionally has been drawn from places where documents have been kept, from persons who were literate, and generally from those using Western European languages. People who were illiterate, such as peasants, or whose writings were not considered worth keeping, such as most women, are mentioned in conventional histories only when literate men judge it necessary to mention them (often disparagingly). Looking at the history of the American fur trade, another problem is highlighted: private businessmen might keep their doings secret to deter competition or avoid interference or taxes. Even if they did not hide their actions deliberately, the only records in public repositories could be bare-bones lists such as ships' bills of lading. Historians and archaeologists must remember that lack of evidence does not prove nothing occurred. Most evidence that a contemporary would have observed is perishable: for example, according to Icelandic sagas, a Vinland colony traded cloth and milk from their cows to Indians in exchange for furs—all perishable. Sixteenth-century European trade into America included quantities of metal and glass beads. For the 1580s spurt of Basque trade, one or two hundred copper kettles and thousands of beads were loaded per ship to exchange for furs, and of these documented from port records, only a handful have been found archaeologically in America. Trying to assess the significance of a 1362 Norse exploration into Minnesota means weighing the low probability of happening to recover identifiable imperishable remains of the expedition. Constructing histories of private persons' affairs is much more challenging than chronicling the politics of European monarchs.

Chapter Nine

The Significance of the Kensington Runestone

If, as seems probable, a party of Swedes and Norwegians got as far as northwestern Minnesota in 1362 with no perceptible effect on world history, why should the record be so dogmatically denied?

An anthropological approach recognizes "popular knowledge" embedded in a society's culture, maintained even when people have learned contrary information. For example, most Americans say that they know that SUVs are safer than passenger automobiles, although published tests show the bigger vehicles are more likely to go out of control and cause accidents. My neighbor tells me he buys pills over the Internet that let him eat to excess and not get fat; somehow he doesn't notice how much weight he's gained over the months he's taken the pill. On college campuses, thousands of supposedly intelligent, literate young adults insist smoking cigarettes will not harm them. These examples show how difficult it can be for even contemporary well-educated Americans to draw valid conclusions from observational data. A study published in 1988 by a team of educational psychologists found, as they put it, "facts do not stand independently of the frames of reference created by the ideological, cultural, and historical contexts in which they arose" (D. Kuhn et al. 1988:216).

Persistent popular interest in the Runestone is labeled "folk archaeology" by a professor of anthropology in northwest Minnesota.

Carrying the "interests" approach to history of science to an extreme, he identifies factors pitting archaeologists against popular beliefs: career-building, necessity to win research grants, and a conviction that professionals' opinion should be authoritative. He emphasizes that archaeologists should respect the economic and self-esteem needs of those Minnesotans who maintain the Runestone Museum and the Catholic Church of Our Lady of the Runestone in Kensington (not a joke) and name motels and shops "Viking." Surprisingly, he accepts unequivocally that the Runestone is a hoax, that it was invented to "justify" Scandinavian immigrants' settlements in Minnesota and now, several generations later, it is a badge for Douglas County businesses. The professor's article in a professional anthropological journal was rebutted by several archaeologists decrying the "anything-goes" attitude. It may not matter to the owner of an auto-body shop whether "Vikings" really were in Douglas County—their descendants certainly were and are. On the other hand, a professor, especially at a state-supported university, is expected to pursue research toward validated knowledge, which includes discerning weak or unsupported arguments, acknowledging difficulties in drawing firm conclusions, and teaching ("professing") what has reasonably been established. Professors should not make fun of people for what they believe, nor should they profess glib admiration for "popular knowledge."

The Kensington Runestone is an anomaly and thus a serious challenge to current knowledge, both popular and academic. So far as we now recognize, if an organized group of Swedes and Norwegians reached Minnesota in 1362, they were as ephemeral as fireflies. Were they a factor in the distinct changes in American Indian societies visible in the late fourteenth century through archaeology? Were they a factor in widespread Atlantic European fifteenth-century businessmen's and aristocrats' explorations? Holding the Runestone's authenticity as a hypothesis may highlight obscured data or suggest new interpretations. Controversies can be very fruitful for science and history.

Einer Haugen, writing in 1942 on the Vinland question, said of the Kensington Runestone:

> The most ambitious runic stone in all America, however, is one
> that has practically no connection with the Vinland voyages, and
> is amazingly remote from the Atlantic seaboard. This is the Kens-
> ington Stone . . . promptly dismissed as a fraud. . . . It contains a

long, narrative inscription of a kind never seen in Scandinavia, written in a strange kind of Swedo-Norwegian, with most unorthodox runic characters, all chiseled with meticulous precision.

Mr. Holand has presented some very plausible arguments in its favor; he has shown that it is not lightly to be dismissed. His notable talent of persuasion and his charm of manner have won him a great following. . . . But he has not yet succeeded in winning over any first-rate authority on runes or medieval Scandinavian languages. The Scandinavian authorities are, in fact, unnecessarily sniffish about it, which may be partly due to a common European suspicion of American frauds. . . . Whether one regards it as spurious or genuine, however, its undeniable presence in Alexandria, Minnesota, is very hard to explain. If it is a hoax, it has not yet been unmasked. (Haugen 1942:156–157)

The Kensington Runestone is the centerpiece in a scientific controversy similar to late-medieval debate about the solar system. Does the system revolve around Earth, or is Earth only one of a set of planets revolving around the Sun? Does the history of the last two millennia revolve around Western Europe, or is Western Europe only part of a global system? Looking at the sixteenth-century controversy over a geocentric versus heliocentric system ("geo-" = earth, "helio-" = sun), we see that anomalies in the movement of astronomical bodies stimulated a few thinkers, particularly Copernicus, to try to change the model of the solar system. Centuries earlier, the famous astronomer Ptolemy had dealt with observations and calculations that stubbornly wouldn't fit his geocentric model by fudging his data. Copernicus, in the early sixteenth century, got more consistent calculations by adjusting the model to make the sun the fixed center. At the beginning of the seventeenth century, Galileo used an explicitly scientific observational method (originally propounded by the Classical Greek scientist Aristotle) to present an Effect (Peirce's "Case"), select a possible Cause (Peirce's "Rule"), then experiment until a reasonable consistency of Results suggested the hypothesized Cause is the probable source of the Effect (or, conversely, is unlikely to be the source). Galileo was quite aware that real situations encompass variables that cannot be controlled, often not even guessed, so experimental results generally will not be in perfect accordance try after try. Galileo's success was due in part to his brilliant ability to figure out practical experiments or, where experiments weren't practical as with motions of planets, find observations (through the recently invented telescope) from the natural world that he could analyze like experiments. His predilection for real-world observations rather than ivory-tower philosophy leads historians to name him "father of modern science."

Another scientific controversy similar to the Runestone is the theory of continental drift. A German meteorologist, Alfred Wegener, presented in 1912 a theory that Africa and South America had been a single continent that broke apart and drifted in opposite directions. Wegener pointed to the outlines of western Africa and eastern South America, which fit like two pieces of a jigsaw puzzle. This had been noticed for a long time; Wegener added data from deep cores he had taken in Greenland showing geological history similar to that in sea-floor corings. A few years later, a South African geologist showed similarities in the geological histories of Africa and South America. Most geologists, particularly Americans, pooh-poohed Wegener's continental drift, asking what mechanism could move continents. A prominent Scottish geologist proposed it could be convection currents he had detected very deep in the earth. This inclined other British geologists to accept the idea of continental drift, while Americans still laughed at the notion. During World War II, the U.S. Navy sponsored massive research on oceans, extending to mapping sea floors and measuring movement in Earth's molten core. Postwar release and discussion of huge amounts of data, coupled with development of computers capable of handling such quantities of data in the 1960s, led even American geologists to accept Wegener's formerly disdained theory—they considered sea-floor spreading to have been demonstrated by the new data, and to be sufficient to account for continental drift. Wegener himself, tragically, died in 1960 in Greenland on another arduous coring expedition.

The history of Wegener's theory is seen as a model of Thomas Kuhn's paradigm shift, beginning with the anomaly of the jigsaw fit of African and South American coastlines, then increasing discrepancy with the old paradigm of stable continents as additional research comes in, supported by technology improvements. For geologists, it was a revolution. There could be a parallel with the theory of Norse in America, with most archaeologists and historians considering the idea no more than a myth until the Ingstads' excavations at L'Anse aux Meadows revealed definitive data demonstrating Norse occupation. The paradigm shifted to acknowledge Norse in the Canadian Maritimes and High Arctic. Nielsen, Hanson, and Wolter expected debate over the Kensington Runestone to be resolved by their new data, physical and historical. Persistent denial indicates something more is involved in acknowledging a party of Goths and Norwegians in Minnesota in 1362. Popular knowledge takes for granted that aliens penetrating into the heartland of America would have world-shaking impact, like Columbus; if they apparently didn't, the account must be a hoax.

Americans have persuaded themselves from the beginning of Anglo colonization in the early seventeenth century that they are an exception to the run of history. Americans believe they live in a New World, whether they think it is a New World granted by God to redeem history, or a New World of Yankee technology freeing us from want and drudgery. The image of an America hanging for five centuries on the northwestern edge of the European world does not fit Americans' conviction that once Europeans became aware of the New World, it became a beacon drawing everyone from intrepid Captain John Smith and General Lafayette to huddled masses yearning to be free. Americans have been taught that their forebears hacked clearings in a virgin wilderness inhabited only by nomadic hunters (remember Laura Ingalls Wilder's *Little House on the Prairie*). We can believe a party of Norse explorers *might* have pushed deep into the wilderness, Daniel Boone style, but if that really happened, how come floods of immigrants didn't follow them? The mythic story of America has two parts: first, there is an Eden-like wilderness America hidden behind a veil of oceans from the active human world, then, Columbus sails to the edge of the world, discovers rich lands ripe to fill Europe's wants, and a neverending boom ensues.

It is a real paradigm shift to believe that the Americas have never been truly isolated. In 1492, when Columbus sailed the ocean blue, a German geographer created the first globe showing the earth as the planet we know. Also in 1492, Topa Inca Yupanqui was nearing the end of his glorious reign over Tawantinsuyu, "the Land of the Four Quarters," stretching from Ecuador into Chile. His merchants sailed the length of the Pacific coast of South America, trading as far north as Mexico. There, the armies of the Lord of the Mexica, Ahuizotl, extended his power over many nations of Mesoamerica, causing tons of tribute to be delivered annually to the magnificent capital, Tenochtitlán, on its web of green canals. Overland trade routes stretched thousands of miles northwestward, through Paquimé on the border of what is now the American

Southwest and on through Nevada to San Francisco Bay. The trans-Mexican trade met the great North Pacific Rim trade system touching Alaska, the Aleutians, Kamchatka, Manchuria, Japan, Korea, and on to China, where it merged with the South Pacific system. In eastern North America, the twelfth-century state with its imposing capital at Cahokia had given way to many small kingdoms from the St. Lawrence Valley to the Gulf of Mexico. Nearly all these regions were flourishing, gaining population, and improving techniques of mass production and shipping of goods.

A world perspective, rather than the usual Eurocentric perspective, shows that in the fifteenth century there was already a world trade system in the northern hemisphere, carried in commercial sailing ships. From northeastern Canada to Greenland and Iceland to Norway, commerce followed the Atlantic coast of Europe, where in Portugal it could branch off to continue along the Atlantic coast of Africa and by 1487 around Africa, or follow the long-established route from Mediterranean ports, especially Venice and Genoa, across that sea to Egypt, through the Red Sea to the Indian Ocean, and via Malaysia and Indonesia to the South China Sea, then through the North Pacific Rim system to British Columbia. There was also the Scandinavians' route, in smaller boats, across northern Russia to Turkey, linking into overland Asian trade routes. The principal American trade system covered South and Middle America into California on the west, where the Pacific coastal trade linked British Columbia and California with inland North America via the Columbia River system, and into eastern North America via the Gulf of Mexico. Yet another system, that of the South Pacific, like the native American system linked tenuously into the Asian segment of the principal world system. What changed in the late fifteenth century was understanding and increasing use of planetary wind patterns, for very good reason usually termed the trade winds, to power trade across, not just around, the Atlantic and Pacific.

This more anthropological perspective accommodates an extended westward journey inland by Norse whose countrymen had been utilizing the entire North Atlantic for centuries. The Kensington Runestone is in the pattern of runestones erected for fallen comrades by Scandinavians in long-distance fur procurement. It is, in this perspective, not an anomaly. Nor is it anomalous that neither American archaeology nor European history documents this privately funded enterprise that could not compete with traditional Scandinavian exploitation of Russian furs. A few centuries later, the Hudson's Bay Company preferred to hire men from Orkney, islands off northern Scotland that had belonged to

Scott Wolter, Jan Wolter, Alice Kehoe, Richard Nielsen, and Barry Hanson at Midwestern/Plains Anthropological Conference, St. Paul, Minnesota, November 2000, soon after Wolter's first laboratory examination of the Runestone in front of him.

Norway. Orkneymen managed well in Canada's forests and water-
ways. The Kensington Runestone party would have lived in the
same cultural tradition, familiar with boats, hunting, hard work,
and life apart from families. From the perspective of Scandinavian
history, we should *expect* at least one entrepreneurial effort to
explore west from Vinland.

The issue comes down, as Thomas Kuhn would have pointed
out, to competing paradigms. One is the myth that the Americas
had been isolated from the historical world until Columbus broke
the barrier in 1492. The other charts world patterns of trade, easily
accommodating a Scandinavian expedition west from Vinland in
1362. Few people, whether scholars or ordinary citizens, are familiar with world trade systems before 1492, whereas everyone early
on was taught that Columbus discovered the New World. It is very
disconcerting to be told that as schoolchildren we innocently
learned biased history. Today, we realize that traditional histories
usually slighted women, lower-class people, and nations conquered
by European empires. It's a step further to move out of a Eurocentric framework, as it was for medieval astronomers to conceptualize
a heliocentric rather than geocentric cosmos.

Will this book persuade scoffers that the weight of probability
now favors the authenticity of the Kensington Runestone inscription? Psychologists have compiled lists of tendencies toward bias:
the strength of early learning or what is learned first; positive or
negative emotional reactions to those presenting data; persever-
ance of belief in spite of information to the contrary; selective mem-
ory such that only belief-sustaining information is recalled;
expectation of certain results, with failure to recognize contrary
data (Miller and Pollock in Shadish and Fuller 1994:243). Dropping
the paradigm of a pristine New World outside of history until
Columbus sailed to the world's edge jolts the structure of beliefs
taught to Americans. Not only does it undermine the idea that the
United States is free of the Old World's tribulations, it deprives
archaeologists of what many view as a great natural experiment,
replication of societal development isolated from any Old World
influences. American nations did develop in their own manner but
that did not preclude occasional contacts with foreign societies, nor
did the fact that European diseases devastated the Americas after
1492 mean that there could not have been earlier contacts unblem-
ished by holocaust (or, in the case of what looks like tuberculosis at

the time of L'Anse aux Meadows, an unrecognized epidemic). The Columbus myth is so entangled with notions of European superiority and American uniqueness that challenges are distressing.

It doesn't matter whether eight Goths and twenty-two Norwegians, and their ten comrades red with blood and dead, were in northwestern Minnesota in 1362. It does matter that educated Americans realize how much of the history they have been taught has been biased. It does matter that Americans understand that authorities can be dogmatic, that good thinking seeks a range of data and carefully weighs probabilities. The significance of a study of the Kensington Runestone is its illumination of struggle between popular knowledge and scientific research. For those who can look at the case, as did Newton Winchell, Robert A. Hall, Jr., and Richard Nielsen, the probability that those Norse were at Kensington is a fruitful hypothesis, collating data in new configurations and opening up intriguing new research questions.

Sources

Chapter 1

Blegen 1968; Hanson 2002; Holand 1932, 1957; Minnesota Historical Society Museum Committee 1910, 1915.

Chapter 2

Betten 1938; Blegen 1968, 1975; Gambino 1993; Gilman and Smith eds. 2000; Holand 1932, 1940, 1946, 1956, 1957, 1962; Kehoe 1990; Kolbert 2002; Lass 1977; Lewis and Loomie 1953; Lunenfeld 1993; Malinowski 1954; Michlovic 1990, 1991; Millett 1999; Pohl 1952; Provost 1992; Sprunger 2000; Sprunger, Susag and Weixel 1998; Wahlgren 1958; Wallace 1999; S. Williams 1991.

Chapter 3

Enterline 2002; Fenton and Pálsson eds. 1984; Fitzhugh and Olin eds. 1993; Gathorne-Hardy 1970; Gibbon 1993, 1994, 1998; Haugen 1942; A. Ingstad 1977; H. Ingstad 1969, 1985, 2001; Jones 1984, 1986; Knarrström 2001; Kurlansky 1999; McGhee 1984; McGhee and Tuck 1977; Michlovic 2001; Mowat 2000; Oleson 1964; Page 1995; Quinn 1974, 1977; Seaver 1996; Sundstrom 2004.

Chapter 4

R. Johnson 2001; Kohlstedt 1999; Merrill 1964; Thrapp 1990; Upham 1915; Weiblen 2002; Winchell 1909; Wolter 2001, 2004.

Chapter 5

Carettini 1983; Eco 1979; Hall 1982, 1994; Hintikka and Hintikka 1983; Hockett 1955; Kuhn 1962, 1970; Nielsen 1998, 1999, 2000, 2002.

Chapter 6

Bowers 1950; Conlogue 2002; Green 1998; Kalm 1972; Murray and Rose 1997; Nyster and O'Connell 1997; Newman 1950; Roberts and Buikstra 2003; Rose and Haron 1999; Salzer and Rajnovich 2001; Science 1999; Smith 1980; Stodder 1999; Wilford 1994; J. Williams 1997.

Chapter 7

Albrecht, ed., 1973; Brønsted 1965; Danielsen et al. 1995; Gjerset 1932[1969]; Larsen 1948; Lloyd 1991; Martin 1986; Nordstrom 2002; Sawyer and Sawyer 1993; Scott 1988.

Chapter 8

Anfinson 1990; Bakker 1989; Barkham 1978; Birk 1994; Blakeslee 1993; Brown and Sasso 2001; Drooker 2002, 2004; Fitzgerald 1992; Gibbon 1993, 1994, 1998; Gregg 1994; Henning 1998; Hollinger and Benn, eds. 1998; C. Johnson 1998; Kuehn 2003; Latta 1992; Lawson 1972; Michlovic and Schneider 1993; Pendergast 2000; Pomeranz 2000; Shay 1990; Tanner 1987; Turgeon 1997, 1998; Williamson and Watts eds. 1999; Wood ed. 1998.

Chapter 9

Barnes 1977, 1982; Barnes, Bloor and Henry 1996; Curtin 1984; Doran 1973; Fernández-Armesto1977; Gladwell 2004; Glen 1982; Hallam 1973, 1989; Kehoe 1998; Kuhn et al. 1988; LeGrand 1988; Machamer et al., eds. 2000; Needham and Lu 1985; Rodgers 1998; Ross 1991; Shadish and Fuller 1994.

Bibliography

Albrecht, Günther, ed. 1973. *Hanse in Europa: Brücke Zwischen den Märk-ten, 12.–17. Jahrhundert.* Cologne: Kölnischen Stadtmuseums.

Anfinson, Scott F. 1990. "Archaeological Regions in Minnesota and the Wood-land Period." In *The Woodland Tradition in the Western Great Lakes: Papers Presented to Elden Johnson,* ed. Guy Gibbon, Publications in Anthropology No. 4, pp. 135–166. Minneapolis: University of Minnesota.

Anonymous. 1999. "The Stories Behind the Bones: Ancient Tuberculosis Identified?" *Science* 286(5442): 1071, 1073–4.

Bakker, Peter. 1989. "Two Basque Loanwords in Micmac." *International Journal of American Linguistics* 55(2): 258–261.

Barkham, Selma. 1978. "The Basques: Filling a Gap in Our History Between Jacques Cartier and Champlain." *Canadian Geographical Journal* 96(1): 8–19.

Barnes, Barry. 1977. *Interests and the Growth of Knowledge.* London: Rou-tledge and Kegan Paul.

———. 1982. *T. S. Kuhn and Social Science.* New York: Columbia Univer-sity Press.

Barnes, Barry, David Bloor, and John Henry. 1996. *Scientific Knowledge: A Sociological Analysis.* Chicago: University of Chicago Press.

Betten, Francis S., SJ. 1938. *From Many Centuries: A Collection of Histor-ical Papers.* New York: P. J. Kennedy & Sons.

Birk, Douglas A. 1994. "When Rivers Were Roads: Deciphering the Role of Canoe Portages in the Western Lake Superior Fur Trade." In *The Fur Trade Revisited: Selected Papers of the Sixth North American Fur Trade Conference, Mackinac Island, Michigan, 1991,* ed. Jennifer S. H. Brown, W. J. Eccles, and Donald P. Heldman, pp. 359–376. East Lan-sing: Michigan State University Press.

Blakeslee, Donald J. 1993. "Modeling the Abandonment of the Central Plains: Radiocarbon Dates and the Origin of the Initial Coalescent." Memoir 27, *Plains Anthropologist* 38(145): 199–214.

Blegen, Theodore C. 1968. *The Kensington Rune Stone: New Light on an Old Riddle.* St. Paul: Minnesota Historical Society.

———. 1975. *Minnesota: A History of the State.* St. Paul: University of Minnesota Press.

Bowers, Alfred W. 1950. *Mandan Social and Ceremonial Organization.* Chicago: University of Chicago Press.

Brøndsted, Johannes. 1971 [1960]. *The Vikings,* trans. Kalle Skov. Harmondsworth: Penguin.

Brown, James A., and Robert F. Sasso. 2001. "Prelude to History on the Eastern Prairies." In *Societies in Eclipse: Archaeology of the Eastern Woodlands Indians, A.D. 1400–1700,* ed. David S. Brose, C. Wesley Cowan, and Robert C. Mainfort, Jr., pp. 205–228. Washington, DC: Smithsonian Institution Press.

Carettini, Gian Paolo. 1983. "Peirce, Holmes, Popper." In *The Sign of Three,* ed. Thomas A. Sebeok and Umberto Eco, pp. 135–153. Bloomington: Indiana University Press.

Conlogue, Gerald. 2002. "More TB in Peruvian Mummies." *Archaeology* 55(2): 14.

Curtin, Philip D. 1984. *Cross-Cultural Trade in World History.* Cambridge: Cambridge University Press.

Danielsen, Rolf, Ståle Dyrvik, Tore Grønlie, Knut Helle, and Edgar Hovland. 1995. *Norway: A History from the Vikings to Our Own Times,* trans. Michael Drake. Oslo: Scandinavian University Press.

Doran, Edwin, Jr. 1973. *Nao, Junk, and Vaka: Boats and Culture History.* College Station: Texas A&M University.

Drooker, Penelope R. 2002. "The Ohio Valley, 1550–1750: Patterns of Sociopolitical Coalescence and Dispersal." In *The Transformation of the Southeastern Indians, 1540–1760,* ed. Robbie Ethridge and Charles Hudson, pp. 115–133. Jackson: University Press of Mississippi.

———. 2004. Contact Period Inter-Regional Trade and Exchange Networks. Paper presented to Society for American Archaeology 69th annual meeting, Montreal.

Eco, Umberto. 1979. *A Theory of Semiotics.* Bloomington: Indiana University Press.

Enterline, James R. 2002. *Erikson, Eskimos and Columbus: Medieval European Knowledge of America.* Baltimore: Johns Hopkins University Press.

Fenton, Alexander, and Hermann Pálsson, eds. 1984. *The Northern and Western Isles in the Viking World: Survival, Continuity and Change.* Edinburgh: John Donald.

Fernández-Armesto, Felipe. 1977. *Before Columbus.* London: Macmillan.

Fitzgerald, William R. 1992. Contact, Contraction, and the Little Ice Age: Neutral Iroquoian Transformation, A.D. 1450–1650. Paper presented to Society for American Archaeology 57th annual meeting, Pittsburgh, PA.

Fitzhugh, William W., and Jacqueline S. Olin, eds. 1993. *Archeology of the Frobisher Voyages*. Washington, DC: Smithsonian Institution Press.

Gambino, Richard. 1993 [1990]. "Revisions of the Christopher Columbus Myth: Is He an Historical Hero?" In *Columbus: Meeting of Cultures*, ed. Mario B. Mignone, Columbus Supplement, pp. 44–50. Stony Brook, NY: Forum Italicum. Reprinted from *Columbus: Modern Views of Columbus and His Time*, ed. Anne and Henry Paolucci, pp. 17–27. Whitestone, NY: Griffon House.

Gathorne-Hardy, Geoffrey M. 1970 [1921]. *The Norse Discoverers of America: The Wineland Sagas Translated and Discussed*. Oxford: Clarendon Press.

Gibbon, Guy. 1993. "The Middle Missouri Tradition in Minnesota: A Review." Memoir 27, *Plains Anthropologist* 38(145): 169–187.

———. 1994. "Cultures of the Upper Mississippi River Valley and Adjacent Prairies in Iowa and Minnesota." In *Plains Indians, A.D. 500–1500*, ed. Karl H. Schlesier, pp. 128–148. Norman: University of Oklahoma Press.

———, ed. 1998. *Archaeology of Prehistoric Native America: An Encyclopedia*. New York: Garland.

Gjerset, Knut 1932 [1969]. *History of the Norwegian People*, vol. 2. New York: AMS Press reprint.

Gilman, Rhoda, and James P. Smith, eds. 2000 [1993]. *Vikings in Minnesota: A Controversial Legacy*. St. Paul: Science Museum of Minnesota Press. Reprint of Minnesota Historical Society Press edition.

Gladwell, Malcolm. 2004. "Big and Bad: How the S.U.V. Ran Over Automotive Safety." *The New Yorker* 79 (January 12): 28–33.

Glen, William. 1982. *The Road to Jaramillo: Critical Years of the Revolution in Earth Science*. Stanford: Stanford University Press.

Green, Roger C. 1998. "Rapahui Origins Prior to European Contact: The View from Eastern Polynesia." In *Easter Island and East Polynesian Prehistory*, ed. P. Vargas Casanova, pp. 87–110. Santiago: Universidad de Chile, Instituto de Estudios Isla de Pascua.

Gregg, Michael L. 1994. "Archaeological Complexes of the Northeastern Plains and Prairie-Woodland Border, A.D. 500–1500." In *Plains Indians, A.D. 500–1500*, ed. Karl H. Schlesier, pp. 71–95. Norman: University of Oklahoma Press.

Hall, Robert A., Jr. 1982. *The Kensington Rune-Stone is Genuine: Linguistic, Practical, Methodological Considerations*. Columbia, SC: Hornbeam Press.

———. 1990. *A Life for Language: A Biographical Memoir of Leonard Bloomfield*. Amsterdam: John Benjamins.

———. 1995. *The Kensington Rune-Stone Authentic and Important: A Critical Edition*. Edward Sapir Monograph Series in Language, Culture, and Cognition, 19. Lake Bluff, IL: Jupiter Press.

Hallam, Anthony. 1973. *A Revolution in the Earth Sciences*. Oxford: Clarendon Press.

———. 1990. *Great Geological Controversies*, 2nd ed. Oxford: Oxford University Press.

Hanson, Barry J. 2002. *Kensington Runestone: A Defense of Olof Ohman the Accused Forger*. Maple, WI: Archaeology ITM.

Haugen, Einar. 1942. *Voyages to Vinland: The First American Saga.* New York: Knopf.

Henning, Dale R. 1998. "The Oneota Tradition." In *Archaeology on the Great Plains*, ed. W. Raymond Wood, pp. 345–414. Lawrence: University Press of Kansas.

Hintikka, Jaako, and Merrill B. Hintikka. 1983. "Sherlock Holmes Confronts Modern Logic: Toward a Theory of Information-Seeking Through Questioning." In *The Sign of Three*, ed. Thomas A. Sebeok and Umberto Eco, pp. 154–169. Bloomington: Indiana University Press.

Hockett, Charles F. 1955. *A Manual of Phonology. Memoir 11 of the International Journal of American Linguistics* 21(4), Part 1. Indiana University Publications in Anthropology and Linguistics. Baltimore: Waverly Press.

Holand, Hjalmar R. 1932. *The Kensington Stone: A Study in Pre-Columbian American History.* Ephraim, WI: Privately printed by Holand.

———. 1940. *Westward from Vinland: An Account of Norse Discoveries and Explorations in America 982–1362.* New York: Duell, Sloan and Pearce.

———. 1946. *America, 1355–1364.* New York: Duell, Sloan and Pearce.

———. 1956. *Explorations in America Before Columbus.* New York: Twayne.

———. 1957. *My First Eighty Years.* New York: Twayne.

———. 1962. *A Pre-Columbian Crusade to America.* New York: Twayne.

Hollinger, R. Eric, and David W. Benn, eds. 1998. "Oneota Taxonomy: Papers from the Oneota Symposium of the 54th Plains Anthropological Conference, 1996." *Wisconsin Archeologist* 79(2).

Ingstad, Anne Stine. 1977. *The Discovery of a Norse Settlement in America: Excavations at L'Anse aux Meadows, Newfoundland 1961–1968.* Oslo: Universitetsforlaget.

———. 1985. *The Norse Discovery of America: The Historical Background and the Evidence of the Norse Settlement Discovered in Newfoundland*, vol. 2. Oslo: Norwegian University Press.

Ingstad, Helge. 1969. *Westward to Vinland: The Discovery of Pre-Columbian Norse House-sites in North America*, trans. Erik J. Friis. London: Jonathan Cape.

———. 2001. *The Viking Discovery of America: The Excavation of a Norse Settlement in L'Anse aux Meadows, Newfoundland.* New York: Checkmark.

Johnson, Craig M. 1998. "The Coalescent Tradition." In *Archaeology on the Great Plains*, ed. W. Raymond Wood, pp. 308–344. Lawrence: University Press of Kansas.

Johnson, Robert G. 2001. Discovery of the AVM Stone. Ms. sent to author.

Jones, Gwyn. 1984. *A History of the Vikings.* Oxford: Oxford University Press.

———. 1986. *The Norse Atlantic Saga: Being the Norse Voyages of Discovery and Settlement to Iceland, Greenland, and North America.* Oxford: Oxford University Press.

Kalm, Peter. 1972. *Travels into North America*, trans. John Reinhold Forster. Barre, MA: Imprint Society.

Kehoe, Alice B. 1990. "Comment on Michlovic's 'On Folk Archaeology in Anthropological Perspective.'" *Current Anthropology* 31(4): 393.

———. 1998. *The Land of Prehistory: A Critical History of American Archaeology.* New York: Routledge.

Knarrström, Bo. 2001. *Flint a Scanian Hardware.* Stockholm, Sweden: National Heritage Board.

Kohlstedt, Sally Gregory. 1999. "Winchell, Newton Horace." In *American National Biography,* ed. John A. Garraty and Mark C. Carnes, vol. 23, pp. 621–622. New York: Oxford University Press.

Kolbert, Elizabeth. 2002. "The Lost Mariner: The Self-Confidence that Kept Columbus Going Was His Undoing." *The New Yorker* 78 (October 14 & 21): 206–211.

Kuehn, Steven R. 2003. A Preliminary Report on Recent Excavation of Three Oneota Sites in Central Wisconsin. Paper presented at Society for American Archaeology annual meeting, Milwaukee, WI.

Kuhn, Deanna, Eric Amsel, and Michael O'Loughlin. 1988. *The Development of Scientific Thinking Skills.* San Diego: Academic Press.

Kuhn, Thomas S. 1970. *The Structure of Scientific Revolutions.* Chicago: University of Chicago Press.

Kurlansky, Mark. 1999. *The Basque History of the World.* New York: Walker.

Larsen, Karen. 1948. *A History of Norway.* Princeton: Princeton University Press.

Lass, William E. 1977. *Minnesota: A Bicentennial History.* New York: W. W. Norton.

Latta, Matha A. 1992. The Influence of European Contact on the 15th-Century Economic Networks in the Great Lakes. Paper presented to the Society for Historical Archaeology annual meeting, Kingston, Jamaica.

Lawson, Murray G. 1972. "The Beaver Hat and the North American Fur Trade." In *People and Pelts: Selected Papers of the Second North American Fur Trade Conference,* ed. Malvina Bolus, pp. 27–37. Winnipeg: Peguis Publishers.

LeGrand, Homer E. 1988. *Drifting Continents and Shifting Theories.* Cambridge: Cambridge University Press.

Lewis, Clifford M., SJ, and Albert J. Loomie, SJ. 1953. *The Spanish Jesuit Mission in Virginia, 1570–1572.* Chapel Hill: University of North Carolina Press.

Lloyd, T. H. 1991. *England and the German Hanse, 1157–1611.* Cambridge: Cambridge University Press.

Lunenfeld, Marvin. 1993. "Columbus-Bashing: Culture Wars over the Construction of an Anti-Hero." In *Columbus: Meeting of Cultures,* ed. Mario B. Mignone, Columbus Supplement, pp. 1–12. Stony Brook, NY: Forum Italicum.

Machamer, Peter, Marcello Pera, and Aristides Baltas, eds. 2000. *Scientific Controversies: Philosophical and Historical Perspectives.* New York: Oxford University Press.

Malinowski, Bronislaw. 1954. *Magic, Science and Religion and Other Essays.* Garden City, NY: Doubleday.

Martin, Janet. 1986. *Treasure of the Land of Darkness: The Fur Trade and Its Significance for Medieval Russia.* Cambridge: Cambridge University Press.

McGhee, Robert. 1984. "Contact Between Native North Americans and the Medieval Norse: A Review of the Evidence." *American Antiquity* 49(1): 4–26.

McGhee, Robert, and James A. Tuck. 1977. "Did the Medieval Irish Visit Newfoundland?" *Canadian Geographic Journal* 94(3): 66–73.

Merrill, George P. 1964. "Winchell, Newton Horace." In *Dictionary of American Biography*, ed. Dumas Malone, vol. 10, pp. 375–376. New York: Charles Scribner's Sons.

Michlovic, Michael G. 1990. "Folk Archaeology in Anthropological Perspective." *Current Anthropology* 31(1): 103–107. See replies by archaeologists in 1990 *Current Anthropology* 31(4): 390–394.

———. 1991. "On Archaeology and Folk Archaeology: A Reply." *Current Anthropology* 32(3): 321–322.

———. 2001. Archaeological Testing at the AVM Locality, Douglas County, Minnesota. Manuscript in possession of Robert G. Johnson, Minnetonka, Minnesota.

Michlovic, Michael G., and Fred E. Schneider. 1993. "The Shea Site: A Prehistoric Fortified Village on the Northeastern Plains." *Plains Anthropologist* 38(143): 117–137.

Millett, Larry. 1999. *Sherlock Holmes and the Rune Stone Mystery*. New York: Penguin.

Minnesota Historical Society. 1915. "The Kensington Runestone—Preliminary Report to the Minnesota Historical Society by its Museum Committee (1910)." *Minnesota Historical Society Collections* XV: 221–286. St. Paul: Minnesota Historical Society.

Mowat, Farley. 2000. *The Farfarers*. South Royalton, VT: Steerforth Press.

Murray, Katherine A., and Jerome C. Rose. 1997. "Bioarcheology of Missouri." In *Bioarcheology of the North Central United States*, ed. Douglas W. Owsley and Jerome C. Rose, Research Series No. 49, pp. 115–146. Fayetteville: Arkansas Archeological Survey.

Museum Committee. 1910. "The Kensington Rune Stone: Preliminary Report to the Minnesota Historical Society." Reprinted in Barry J. Hanson, *Kensington Runestone: A Defense of Olof Ohman the Accused Forger*, vol. 2, A 2, Facsimile pp. 221–286. Maple, WI: Archaeology ITM.

Myster, Susan M. Thurston, and Barbara O'Connell. 1997. "Bioarcheology of Iowa, Wisconsin, and Minnesota." In *Bioarcheology of the North Central United States*, ed. Douglas W. Owsley and Jerome C. Rose, Research Series no. 49, pp. 147–239. Fayetteville: Arkansas Archeological Survey.

Needham, Joseph, and Lu Gwei-djen. 1985. *Trans-Pacific Echoes and Resonances: Listening Once Again*. Singapore: World Scientific.

Newman, Marshall T. 1950. "The Blond Mandan: A Critical Review of an Old Problem." *Southwestern Journal of Anthropology* 6:255–272.

Nielsen, Richard. 1998. "Linguistic Aspects Concerning the Kensington Runestone." *Epigraphic Society Occasional Papers* 23:189–265.

———. 1999. "New Discoveries Concerning the Kensington Runestone and Other North American Runic Inscriptions." *Epigraphic Society Occasional Papers* 23.

———. 2000. "Early Scandinavian Incursions into the Western States." *Journal of the West* 39(1): 72–86.

———. 2002. "The Kensington Rune Stone and Evidence in *Erikskrönikan,* Mid-14th Century Diplomas, and the Kingigtorssuaq Inscription." In Barry J. Hanson, *Kensington Runestone: A Defense of Olof Ohman the Accused Forger,* Appendix D, pp. D1–45. Maple, WI: Archaeology ITM.

Nilsestuen, Rolf M. 1994. *The Kensington Runestone Vindicated.* Lanham, MD: University Press of America.

Nordstrom, Byron J. 2002. *The History of Sweden.* Westport, CT: Greenwood Press.

Oleson, Tryggvi J. 1964. *Early Voyages and Northern Approaches 1000–1632.* Toronto: McClelland and Stewart.

Page, R. I. 1995. *Chronicles of the Vikings: Records, Memorials and Myths.* London: British Museum Press.

Pendergast, James F. 2000. "The Identity of Stadacona and Hochelaga: Comprehension and Conflict." In *Interpretations of Native North American Life: Material Contributions to Ethnohistory,* ed. Michael S. Nassaney and Eric S. Johnson, pp. 53–87. Gainesville: University Press of Florida.

Peterson, C. Stewart. 1946. *America's Rune Stone of A.D. 1362 Gains Favor.* New York: Hobson Book Press.

Pohl, Frederick J. 1952. *The Lost Discovery: Uncovering the Track of the Vikings in America.* New York: W. W. Norton.

Pomeranz, Kenneth. 2000. *The Great Divergence: China, Europe, and the Making of the Modern World Economy.* Princeton: Princeton University Press.

Provost, Foster. 1992. "Review Essay on Margarita Zamora's *Reading Columbus.*" *1992: A Columbus Newsletter* 16: 1–4.

Quinn, David B. 1974. *England and the Discovery of America, 1481–1620.* London: Allen and Unwin.

———. 1977. *North America from Earliest Discoveries to First Settlements: The Norse Voyages to 1612.* New York: Harper & Row.

Roberts, Charlotte A., and Jane E. Buikstra. 2003. *The Bioarchaeology of Tuberculosis.* Gainesville: University Press of Florida.

Rodgers, Daniel T. 1998. "Exceptionalism." In *Imagined Histories: American Historians Interpret the Past,* ed. Anthony Molho and Gordon S. Wood, pp. 21–40. Princeton: Princeton University Press.

Rose, Jerome C., and Anna M. Harmon. 1999. "Louisiana and South and Eastern Arkansas." In *Bioarcheology of the South Central United States,* ed. Jerome C. Rose, Research Series No. 55, pp. 35–82. Fayetteville: Arkansas Archeological Survey.

Ross, Dorothy. 1991. *The Origins of American Social Science.* Cambridge: Cambridge University Press.

Salzer, Robert J., and Grace Rajnovich. 2001. *The Gottschall Rockshelter: An Archaeological Mystery,* rev. ed. St. Paul, MN: Prairie Smoke Press.

Sawyer, Birgit, and Peter Sawyer. 1993. *Medieval Scandinavia: From Conversion to Reformation, circa 800–1500.* Minneapolis: University of Minnesota Press.

Scott, Franklin D. 1988. *Sweden: The Nation's History*. Carbondale: South-ern Illinois University Press.

Seaver, Kirsten A. 1996. *The Frozen Echo: Greenland and the Exploration of North America, ca. A.D. 1000–1500*. Stanford: Stanford University Press.

Shadish, William R., and Steve Fuller, eds. 1994. *The Social Psychology of Science*. New York: Guilford Press.

Shay, C. Thomas. 1990. "Perspectives on the Late Prehistory of the North-eastern Plains." In *The Woodland Tradition in the Western Great Lakes: Papers Presented to Elden Johnson*, ed. Guy Gibbon, Publications in Anthropology No. 4, pp. 113–133. Minneapolis: University of Minnesota.

Smith, G. Hubert. 1980. *The Explorations of the La Vérendryes in the Northern Plains, 1738–43*. Lincoln: University of Nebraska Press.

Sprunger, David A. 2000. "J. A. Holvik and the Kensington Runestone." *Minnesota History* 57 (Fall): 141–154.

Sprunger, David, Peter Susag, and Elizabeth Weixel. 1998. *J. A. Holvik and the Kensington Runestone: A Study in Ethnic, Religious, and Com-munity Identity*. Moorhead, MN: Concordia College.

Stodder, Ann Lucy Wiener. 1999. "Basin and Range." In *Bioarcheology of the South Central United States*, ed. Jerome C. Rose, Research Series No. 55, pp. 184–220. Fayetteville: Arkansas Archeological Survey.

Sundstrom, Linea. 2004. *Storied Stone: Indian Rock Art of the Black Hills Country*. Norman: University of Oklahoma Press.

Tanner, Helen Hornbeck, ed. 1987. *Atlas of Great Lakes Indian History*. Norman: University of Oklahoma Press.

Thrapp, Dan L. 1990. "Winchell, Newton Horace." In *Encyclopedia of Fron-tier Biography*, ed. Dan L. Thrapp, vol. 3, pp. 1581–1582. Spokane, WA: Arthur H. Clark.

Turgeon, Laurier. 1997. "The Tale of the Kettle: Odyssey of an Intercul-tural Object." *Ethnohistory* 44(1): 1–19.

———. 1998. "French Fishers, Fur Traders, and Amerindians During the Sixteenth Century: History and Archaeology." *William and Mary Quarterly*, third series 55(4): 585–610.

Upham, Warren. 1915. "Memoir of Newton Horace Winchell." *Geological Society of America Bulletin* 26:27–31.

Wahlgren, Erik. 1958. *The Kensington Stone: A Mystery Solved*. Madison: University of Wisconsin Press.

Wallace, Anthony F. C. 1999. *Jefferson and the Indians: The Tragic Fate of the First Americans*. Cambridge, MA: Belknap.

Weiblen, Paul W. 2002. "Report on a Partial Mineralogical Characteriza-tion of the Kensington Rune Stone." In Barry J. Hanson, *Kensington Runestone: A Defense of Olof Ohman the Accused Forger*, vol. 2, pp. H1–H45. Maple, WI: Archaeology ITM.

Wilford, John Noble. 1994. "Tuberculosis Found to Be Old Disease in New World." *New York Times* (March 15): B5, B10.

Williams, John A. 1997. "Bioarcheology of the Northeastern Plains." In *Bioarcheology of the North Central United States*, ed. Douglas W. Ows-ley and Jerome C. Rose, Research Series No. 49, pp. 57–87. Fay-etteville: Arkansas Archeological Survey.

Williams, Stephen. 1991. *Fantastic Archaeology*. Philadelphia: University of Pennsylvania Press.

Williamson, Ronald F., and Christopher M. Watts, ed. 1999. *Taming the Taxonomy: Toward a New Understanding of Great Lakes Archaeology*. Toronto: eastendbooks.

Winchell, Newton H. 1909. "The Kensington Rune Stone." Report read before Minnesota Historical Society, December 13, 1909. Facsimile printed in Barry J. Hanson, *Kensington Runestone: A Defense of Olof Ohman the Accused Forger*, vol. 2, pp. A1–11. Maple, WI: Archaeology ITM.

Wolter, Scott F. 2001. "Kensington Runestone Observations, APS Job #10–0112.0." Ms. Report. St. Paul, MN: American Petrographic Services.

———. 2004a. "The Geology of the Kensington Rune Stone." Ms. Report. St. Paul, MN: American Petrographic Services.

———. 2004b "Response to Runo Löfvendahl's Comments on Wolter Report on the Kensington Rune Stone." Ms. Report. St. Paul, MN: American Petrographic Services.

Wood, W. Raymond, ed. 1998. *Archaeology on the Great Plains*. Lawrence: University Press of Kansas.

Index

Anishinaabe (Ojibwa, Chippewa), 74
Anthropology, four subfields, 51
Arctic, Norse in, 27, 67
Assiniboin, 73
AVM Stone, 22, 35–36
Aztalan, 60
Aztec (Mexica), 83
Barnes, Barry, 40
Black Death, 15, 63
Blegen, Theodore, 12
"Blond" hair among American Indians, 55
Bloomfield, Leonard, and scientific linguistics, 33, 42
Breda, Olaus, 4, 11
Cahokia, prehistoric city, 60, 74
Catlin, George, 58
Chaco Canyon, 54, 74
Cheyenne, 73
Conference, Plains Anthropological and Midwest Archaeological, 15, 34
Cree, 76
Crow Creek, S.D., 72–73
Curme, George, 4
Dakota, 72–73, 74
Fitzhugh, William, 14, 44
Flaten, Nils, 3, 12
Flom, George, 7–8, 11
Frobisher, Martin, and Arctic expedition, 1576–1578, 28–29
Giants, legendary antagonists of Ho-Chunk, 59–60

Gibbon, Guy, 15, 71
Gottschall Rock Shelter, 58
Greenland, 16, 26
Hagen, Sivert, 42
Hall, Charles, 28
Hall, Robert A., Jr., 33, 41–44, 46
Hanse (Hanseatic League), 15, 63–64, 65
Hanson, Barry, 14, 34
Harrison, Christina, 22
Haugen, Einar, 80
Hidatsa, 56, 73
History, problems in discovering data, 78
Ho-Chunk, 58, 74
Hockett, Charles, 44–45
Hoegh, Knut, 7
Holand, Hjalmar, 4–7, 9, 11–12, 31, 41, 57
Holvik, J. A., 40
Hotchkiss, William, 32
Hudson's Bay Company, compared to medieval Norse, 68–69
Inca Empire, 83
Ingstad, Helge, 18, 23–24
Ingstad, Anne Stine, 18, 23–25, 26
Ioway, 73, 74
Iroquoians, 75
Johnson, Robert, 36
Kalm, Peter (Pehr), 57
Kansa, 7
Kensington, Minnesota, 68
Kingiktorsuag Runestone, 27

Knutson, Paul (Pál Knutsson), 16
Kuhn, Thomas (*Structure of
    Scientific Revolutions*), 39–40,
    45, 82, 86
L'Anse aux Meadows, 18, 23–26, 75
Löfvendahl, Runo, 38
Madoc, legendary prince of Wales, 55
Magnus Eiriksson, 16, 64–65
Mandan, 55–58, 73
Maximilian, Prince of Wied, visiting
    Mandans, 58
Michlovic, Michael, 22
Minnesota Historical Society, 8, 22, 32
Minnesota State Archaeological
    Survey zones, 71
Missouri, 74
Montelius, Oscar, 9–10
Myth, societal chartering, 17, 83, 86
Newport Tower, R.I., claimed to be
    medieval Norse, 10
Nielsen, Richard, 12–15, 34, 44, 47
Ohman, Olof, 3, 6–7, 9, 32, 41
Ojakangas, Richard, 36
Ojibwa, *see Anishinaabe*
Oneota (prehistoric culture), 72
Omaha, 74
Osage, 74
Oto, 73, 74
Paquimé, 83
Ponca, 74
Patton, LuAnn, 34
Peirce, Charles, on scientific logic, 45
    book, *The Sign of Three*,
        explaining Peirce's logic, 47
Peru, tuberculosis in prehistoric
    populations, 52, 54
"Popular" or "folk" knowledge, 79, 83,
    87
Psinomani (prehistoric Dakota), 71
Pueblos, tuberculosis in prehistoric
    populations, 52
Quapaw, 74
Red Horn, Ho-Chunk hero, 58–60
Runes, in medieval Scandinavia, 43
Runestone, Kensington, description
    of stone, 34–35
    inscription, with translation, 48–49
    logical analysis of inscription, 46

Sacajawea and Lewis and Clark
    expedition, 56
Salzer, Robert, 60
Scandinavia, medieval kings and
    politics, 65
Science, anomalies and controversies
    in, 45–47, 81–82
    psychological biases influencing,
        86
Siouan First Nations, 73, 74
Spanish colonists, known to Plains
    Indians, 57
Stone tools, 30
Storms-As-He-Walks, Ho-Chunk
    thunderbird, 58–59
Sundstrom, Linéa, 22
Tanner, Helen Hornbeck, 68
Toltec (Mexican nation), 74
Tombstones, in Maine and
    Wisconsin, 37
Trade, in prehistoric and
    protohistoric America, 54, 72, 75
    fur trade, 17, 28, 66, 73, 75, 77, 78,
        86
    fifteenth-century world routes, 84
    North Pacific Rim routes, 84
Tuberculosis (*Mycobacterium
    tuberculosis*), 52–55, 87
    in Pleistocene bison, 53
Turner, Frederick Jackson, 5
Upham, Warren, 8, 12, 32
Vair, Russian northern squirrel fur,
    66
    Cinderella's slippers made of, 69
Vérendrye, Pierre Gaultier, 57
Viking, defined, 63
Vikings: The North Atlantic Saga, 43
Vinland, 18–19
Wahlgren, Erik, 41
Wallace, Birgitta Lineroth, 26, 44
Wegener, Alfred, 82
Weiblen, Paul, 36
Westin, Janey Johnson, 36
Winchell, Newton H., 8, 12, 31–32,
    41, 47
Wolter, Scott, 14, 23, 34–38